遠藤
MINARI
ENDOH
海

Dazzle Vol. 2

Created by Minari Endoh

Translation - Yoohae Yang
English Adaptation - Peter Ahlstrom
Copy Editor - Peter Ahlstrom
Retouch and Lettering - Alyson Stetz
Production Artist - Fawn Lau
Cover Design - Gary Shum

Editor - Troy Lewter
Digital Imaging Manager - Chris Buford
Managing Editor - Lindsey Johnston
Editor-in-Chief - Rob Tokar
VP of Production - Ron Klamert
Publisher - Mike Kiley
President and C.O.O. - John Parker
C.E.O. and Chief Creative Officer - Stuart Levy

A  Manga

TOKYOPOP Inc.
5900 Wilshire Blvd. Suite 2000
Los Angeles, CA 90036

E-mail: info@TOKYOPOP.com
Come visit us online at www.TOKYOPOP.com

ISBN: 1-59816-093-1

First TOKYOPOP printing: May 2006

10 9 8 7 6 5 4 3 2 1

Printed in the USA

DAZZLE

Vol. 2

Minari Endoh

HAMBURG // LONDON // LOS ANGELES // TOKYO

Story So Far...

A young girl named Rahzel with magical abilities is abruptly sent off to see the world by her father. At first she is alone on her journey...until she meets Alzeid, a mysterious lone traveler who has abilities similar to hers. He is on a mission to find his father's killer...and even though they initially don't get along, the two become traveling companions, helping each other on their respective journeys. They encounter various people throughout their travels, and take it upon themselves to help the downtrodden and right wrongs (for the right amount of cash, of course). Things were actually going well...until they crossed paths with Soresta and Baroqueheat, two old acquaintances of Alzeid's who are escorting a young boy named Vincent on his journey to his family. They ask Alzeid to join them and help them make money...but he refuses. Their crassness aside, Rahzel's suspicions that all three are hiding something is only deepened after she and Vincent are attacked by professional hit men. She declares her distrust of them all...and it appears that the once blossoming partnership is now wilting.

Contents

THERE'S GONNA BE A FIGHT!
THE CHAMP FROM PLATOON TWO'S FIGHTIN' THE ROOKIE!
I'M TAKING ALL BETS!
DID YA HEAR? WHO'RE YOU GONNA BET ON?
THOUGH MAYBE WE SHOULD CHECK THEM OUT FIRST, HUH?
I DON'T HAVE ANY MONEY TO BET WITH RIGHT NOW.
BETTING MY LIFE'S A LUCRATIVE PLAN IF I WIN, BUT IF I LOSE, I'LL BE FORCED TO KILL EVERYONE AND BECOME A FUGITIVE...
...OR YOU COULD JUST ASK ME TO SPOT YOU SOME...
DOESN'T MATTER.
HMM... SHALL I BET MY LIFE ON THE ROOKIE?
HUH?

Chapter 8:
Nowhere to Go--Part 3: Like Praying

SO, WHAT DO YOU THINK, ALZEID?
ABOUT WHAT?
ABOUT THAT CONVERSATION YESTERDAY!
YOU'VE GOT US ALL WRONG.

I ALREADY EXPLAINED TO YOU ABOUT HOW VINCENT'S AN ILLEGITIMATE CHILD FROM SOME WEALTHY FAMILY.

THEY'VE GOT A BIG DISPUTE CENTERED ON HIM RIGHT NOW.
I DIDN'T TELL YOU THE DETAILS BECAUSE I DON'T WANT TO MAKE TROUBLE FOR YOU.

DOESN'T IT SMELL FISHY?
THEY'RE SUPPOSED TO BE VEE'S BODY-GUARDS.
SO HOW COME THEY'RE ALWAYS LEAVING VEE BY HIMSELF?
They're just goofing off on their own!

IF YOU CAN'T TRUST THEM, DON'T GET INVOLVED.
Wah!
TOO LATE FOR THAT...
...'CAUSE I ALREADY DECIDED...
...THAT I'M FOLLOWING THEM TO OBPLAY.

ずるずる
Drag
?
IT WAS NICE KNOWING YOU.
I'M SORRY! I SHOULD'VE ASKED YOUR OPINION FIRST!
BUT IT'S YOUR FAULT FOR HAVING SHADY FRIENDS LIKE THEM IN THE FIRST PLACE!
I HAVE NO OBLIGATION TO TAKE RE-SPONSIBILITY FOR ANYONE ELSE.
WELL, WE CAN TALK ABOUT IT LATER.
RIGHT NOW WE NEED MORE TRAINING!
Hey! Come on!
DON'T THINK I DIDN'T NOTICE YOU CHANGING THE SUB-JECT...
...BUT FINE.
わくわく

I'VE GOT MY OWN QUES-TION...
YOU'RE THE ONE WHO ASKED TO MEET ME HERE FOR TRAIN-ING.
WHY THE HECK DID YOU SHOW UP IN THAT GIRLY OUTFIT?!
I WANTED TO COM-PETE WITH YOUR MAID COSTUME FROM THAT PHOTO.
THE THEME IS "PRINCE" ...
By the way, this horse is Johnny...
...an optional accessory.
YOU DON'T HAVE TO COMPETE!
Put the horse away!
DON'T YOU KNOW...
Huh?
...YOU DON'T HAVE TO KEEP A PROMISE IN A SITUATION LIKE THAT?

IF YOU'RE IN REAL DANGER, JUST GO AHEAD AND USE YOUR MAGICAL POWER.
DON'T CAUSE PROBLEMS FOR OTHER PEOPLE.
IS HE MAD AT ME?!
You're the one who told me not to use my power!

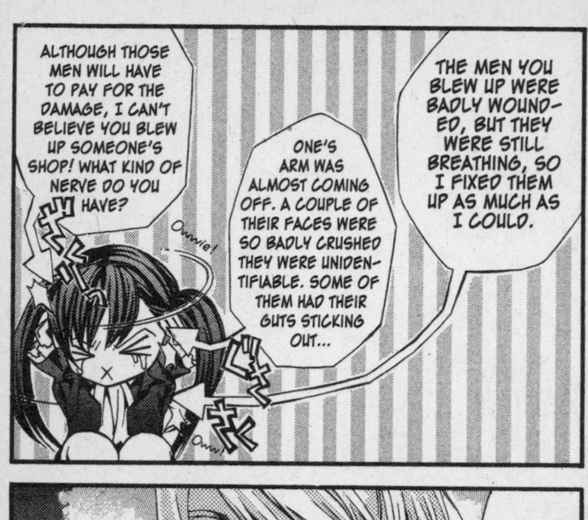
THE MEN YOU BLEW UP WERE BADLY WOUNDED, BUT THEY WERE STILL BREATHING, SO I FIXED THEM UP AS MUCH AS I COULD.
ONE'S ARM WAS ALMOST COMING OFF. A COUPLE OF THEIR FACES WERE SO BADLY CRUSHED THEY WERE UNIDENTIFIABLE. SOME OF THEM HAD THEIR GUTS STICKING OUT...
ALTHOUGH THOSE MEN WILL HAVE TO PAY FOR THE DAMAGE, I CAN'T BELIEVE YOU BLEW UP SOMEONE'S SHOP! WHAT KIND OF NERVE DO YOU HAVE?
Owwie!
Oww!
ARE YOU IN SUCH A HURRY...
...TO BECOME A KILLER?

BUT I'M STILL GONNA KEEP MY PROMISE!
I WON'T USE MY POWER FOR ANOTHER SIX DAYS!
I SWEAR IT!
POINT TAKEN.

TO TELL YOU THE TRUTH...
...THIS ISN'T THE FIRST TIME I'VE HAD TO TRY NOT USING MY POWER.
MY FATHER USED TO SAY, "YOU MUST BE ABLE TO DO THINGS WITHOUT YOUR MAGICAL POWER...
RAHZEL! I MADE YOU A LUNCH! LET'S GO HIKING!
It's a big, fancy, five-layered lunchbox!
Ehh?!
I've got school today!
...BECAUSE YOU NEVER KNOW WHEN YOU COULD LOSE YOUR POWER."
Just taste that mountain air!
Are you drugged outta your mind?!
BUT I COULDN'T EVEN *IMAGINE* LOSING MY POWER.
THIS IS FOR YOUR PROTECTION.
DO YOUR BEST TO CLIMB DOWN THE MOUNTAIN...
Wha?!
...BY YOURSELF, OKAY?
IF YOU USE YOUR MAGICAL POWER BEFORE YOU GET HOME, I'LL HANG MY-SELF, GOT IT?
Bye-bye, now!!
Wait! Dad!
IT WAS A SURPRISE MAGIC BAN.
Ha!

IT WAS SO DARK THAT I COULDN'T SEE. MY COMPASS STOPPED WORKING, AND A STRANGE CREATURE WAS TRACKING ME. I CRIED ALL THE WAY DOWN THE MOUNTAIN.
Waaah! Where am I?!
I'm starving!
THE MEMORY GIVES ME NIGHTMARES EVEN NOW.
WHAT WAS THE STRANGE CREATURE?
I wanna see.
↑His eyes are out of focus.
YOUR FATHER IS RATHER... UNIQUE.
BUT I LATER FOUND OUT THAT EVERY TIME HE TESTED ME LIKE THAT, HE WAS FOLLOWING ME STEALTHILY.
I COULD TELL HE WAS REALLY NERVOUS AND WORRIED ABOUT ME.
IT WAS SO FUNNY!
HE'S *SO* OVERPROTECTIVE!

BUT YOU'VE GOTTA RESCUE ME...

...WHEN-EVER I'M IN REAL DANGER, OKAY?

I HOPE YOU'RE NOT LOOKING FOR THE SAME KIND OF PROTEC-TION FROM ME.

I DON'T WANT YOU TO STALK ME, EITHER.

AND I'LL RESCUE YOU...

...WHEN YOU NEED ME TO, ALZEID.

...
HMPH.

WHAT COULD YOU DO TO RESCUE ME?
OW, OW! YOU'RE PULLING MY ARM OUT OF ITS SOCKET!
IT DOESN'T COUNT IF YOU BEAT ME LIKE THAT!

HEY, ALZEID, RAHZEL!
I'm sleepy...
THE HOTEL MANAGER IS COMPLAINING THAT YOU GUYS ARE BEING TOO NOISY.

OH.

YOU GUYS SHOULD CALL ME WHEN YOU'RE GONNA DO SOMETHING LIKE THAT!
Alzeid! Such a wild animal!
HOW'D YOU LIKE ME TO GIVE YOU A NICE BROKEN NECK?

WELL, I'M WORN OUT.
I'M GOING TO HIT THE SHOWER. WHY DON'T YOU PLAY WITH THIS GUY INSTEAD?

SCHFF
HOLD ON!
WHY DO I HAVE TO PLAY WITH *HIM?!*

GET THE HELL OUT OF HERE!
Do you hate me that much?

Mmm.♪
I'D BE HAPPY TO TAKE HIS SUGGES-TION.
WHAT ARE YOU UP FOR? PHYSICAL TRAIN-ING?
I COULD TEACH YOU A LITTLE SOME-THING YOU'VE NEVER DONE BEFORE...

SO QUICK TO ANSWER!
I DETEST YOU!
You've got three seconds to scram before I kill you.
AND SHE EVEN THREATENS ME!!
I don't know what to do with her anymore!

LIKE I SAID, I CAN'T TRUST YOU!
AND ALSO... I MAY SOUND PREJUDICED...
...BUT I CAN'T HELP THINKING OF THE ARMY AS A BUNCH OF KILLERS.

AREN'T YOU CURIOUS ABOUT WHY ALZEID USED TO BE ONE OF THOSE "KILLERS"?

I DON'T CARE!
SHE'S SO SIMPLE-MINDED.

BUT I AL-READY QUIT THE ARMY, UNLIKE SORESTA.
SO FEEL FREE TO JUMP INTO MY--♡
YOU WERE STILL ONE OF THEM!
Jump into where?!

I LIED. ACTUALLY, I WANT TO KNOW THAT MORE THAN ANYTHING.
BUT I DON'T WANNA HEAR FROM YOU.
I WANT TO HEAR IT STRAIGHT FROM THE HORSE'S MOUTH.
THERE'S ALSO A LOT OF STUFF I HAVEN'T TOLD ALZEID YET, EITHER.

Ahh...
I HAD NO IDEA.
I ASSUMED YOU WERE TELLING HIM EVERYTHING ABOUT YOURSELF.
I'M NOT IN THE HABIT OF DIVULGING ANYTHING WITHOUT BEING ASKED.
Don't make it sound like I have a big mouth!

IN THE OBPLAY ARMY WE USED TO BELONG TO, EVEN SOMEONE WITH NO IDENTI-FICATION COULD JOIN UP.
AND AFTER SOLDIERS SERVED ON ACTIVE DUTY FOR A WHILE, THEY WERE PROVIDED WITH AN OF-FICIAL FAMILY REGISTRY.
WITH THAT REGISTRY, EVEN PEOPLE LIKE US COULD TRAVEL BETWEEN COUNTRIES.
ALZEID WANTED REVENGE ON HIS FATHER'S MURDERER.
IT WAS ALL...
BUT HE COULDN'T DO THAT WITHOUT BEING ABLE TO TRAVEL.
...FOR REVENGE.
SO HE DEVOTED THE BLOSSOM OF HIS YOUTH TO PREPAR-ING FOR HIS REVENGE.

TOO DE-
PRESS-
ING!
I APPRE-
CIATE THAT
YOU SHARED
SUCH IMPOR-
TANT INFOR-
MATION!
BUT
TALKATIVE
MEN LIKE
YOU JUST
CAN'T BE
POPULAR
AMONG
GIRLS!
SEE YA!
SLAM!
creak
THE
WAY YOU'RE
DRESSED,
YOU'RE GONNA
CATCH A COLD
OUT THERE.
Click
ALZEID
IS SO
STUPID!

WHY'S HE SO STUCK ON GETTING REVENGE FOR HIS FATHER?
HE SHOULDN'T HAVE WASTED SO MUCH TIME PLANNING THIS REVENGE.
IT'S IDIOTIC THAT HE'S SPENT YEARS AND YEARS JUST GETTING READY!
CAN'T HE JUST APPRECIATE THAT HE STILL HAS HIS OWN LIFE?!
AH!
RAHZEL!
HE'S A MORON!
HEY, I NEED TO TALK TO YOU ABOUT SOME-THING...
EVEN MUAY THAI ARTISTS WOULD SEE WHAT A WASTE HE IS!
Big Public Bath
She's not listening to me.
A TRUE IDIOT!
ALZEID !!

ぎょ。

Huh?

HEY...THIS IS THE MEN'S ROOM.
LET'S PLAY!
Getting dressed.

YOU'RE GOING TO HANG OUT WITH A PRETTY GIRL! YOU'RE GONNA TAKE HER OUT TO EAT AND GO SHOPPING WITH HER!
?
AND YOU'RE GOING TO GET EXHAUSTED FROM LAUGHING ABOUT STUPID STUFF!

WHO PLAYS THE PRETTY GIRL?
MOI!
......

IT MAY SOUND LIKE A WASTE OF TIME TO YOU...
...BUT TIMES LIKE THIS CAN BE A VERY IMPORTANT SOURCE OF POWER!
I WANT TO GIVE HIM BACK THE TIME HE LOST.
THIS IS *CRITICAL* FOR *YOU!*
THE LEAST I CAN DO IS TRY TO HELP HIM.

I'LL BE BACK IN TEN MINUTES. JUST WAIT FOR ME.
SAY, "YES, SIR!"
YEAH!!
WHAT KIND OF ANSWER IS THAT?!
WELCOME HOME, ALZEID! I HEARD YOU WERE BACK!

YOU WANNA EAT SOME DINNER TOGETHER?
SORRY. I ALREADY ATE.
WHY WOULD I WANT TO HAVE DINNER WITH ANOTHER MAN, ANYWAY?
BUT YOUR TIMING IS GOOD.
I THOUGHT SHE HATED US.
Heh heh...
THIS IS A SOUVENIR FROM RAHZEL.
SHE SAID YOU SHOULD EAT IT WITH BAROQUE-HEAT.
SHE WAS WORRIED THAT YOU GUYS WERE STARVING AND WAITING FOR US.

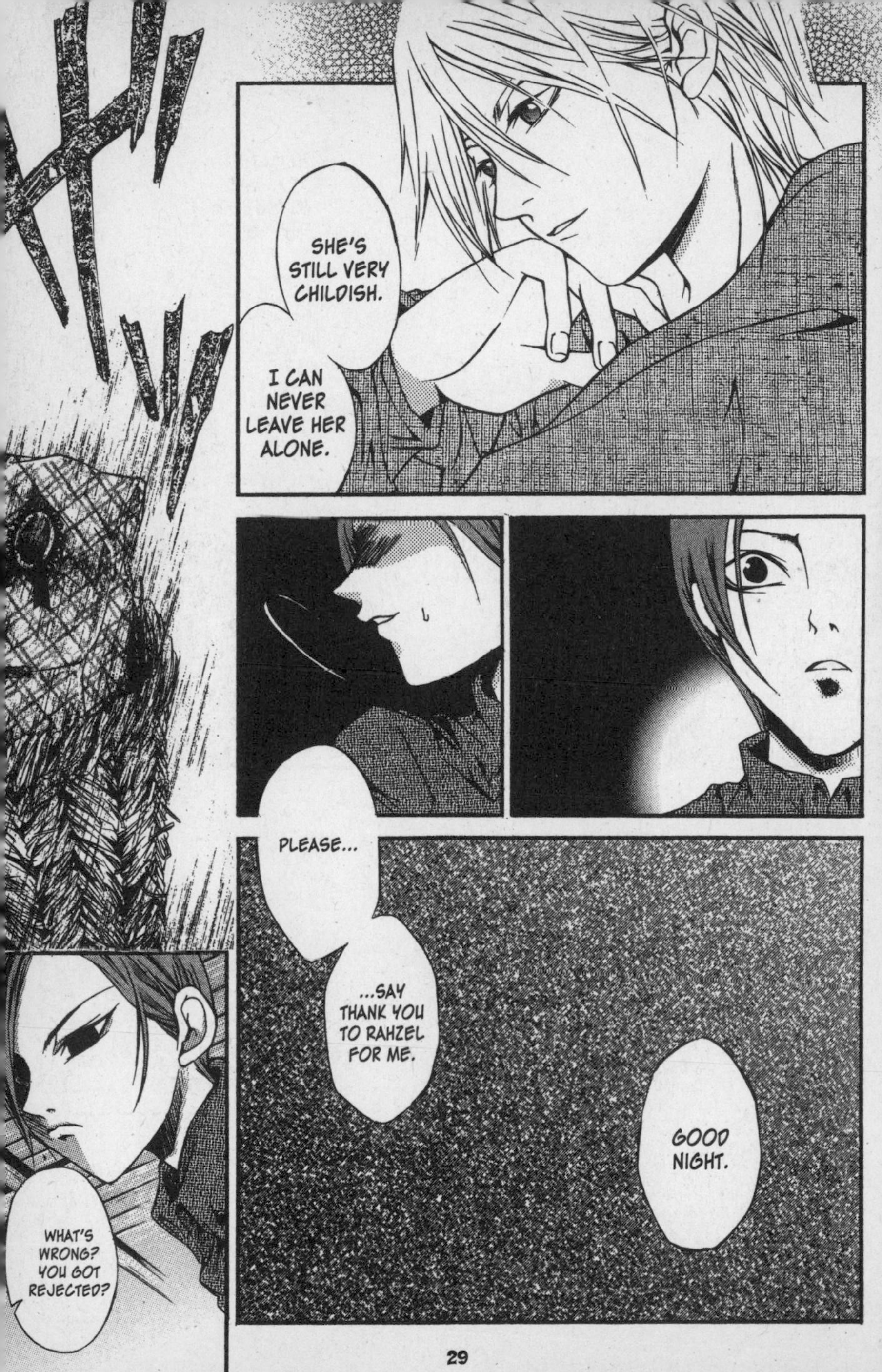
SHE'S STILL VERY CHILDISH.
I CAN NEVER LEAVE HER ALONE.
PLEASE...
...SAY THANK YOU TO RAHZEL FOR ME.
GOOD NIGHT.
WHAT'S WRONG? YOU GOT REJECTED?

DON'T TAKE IT OUT ON ME.
SHUT UP!

WELL, WELL...

I'M GONNA GO BACK TO THE ROOM, NOW.

は
Sigh...
JUST TELL ME YOU DON'T WANT IT, AND I'LL EAT IT.
WHAT ARE YOU TALKING ABOUT?

IT'S A SECRET. ♡
DID YOU JUST TAKE A SHOWER?
You smell good! ♥
ぷっ
BUZZ OFF!!

RAHZEL!
THANKS FOR THE FOOD!
A NOTE?
I'd like to discuss something important with you.
Please come see me at the park by the hotel.
HEY! VEE!
VINCENT!

THAT'S ODD...
IS THERE SOME OTHER PARK AROUND HERE?
Rustle

WHO'S THERE?!
WHOA!
BAROQUE-HEAT?

DIDN'T I SAY NOT TO REACT VIOLENTLY WITHOUT FIRST CHECKING WHO IT IS?
STOP SNEAKING UP BEHIND ME, THEN!
WHY ARE YOU OUT HERE, ANYWAY?

I WANTED TO CHECK OUT THE COUPLES DOING THE NASTY IN THE PARK LATE AT NIGHT.
DIS-GUSTING!
You are the dirtiest man I've ever met!

WELL, ENJOY THE SHOW.
OH...I FORGOT TO MENTION THAT VIN-CENT ISN'T COMING.

EH?

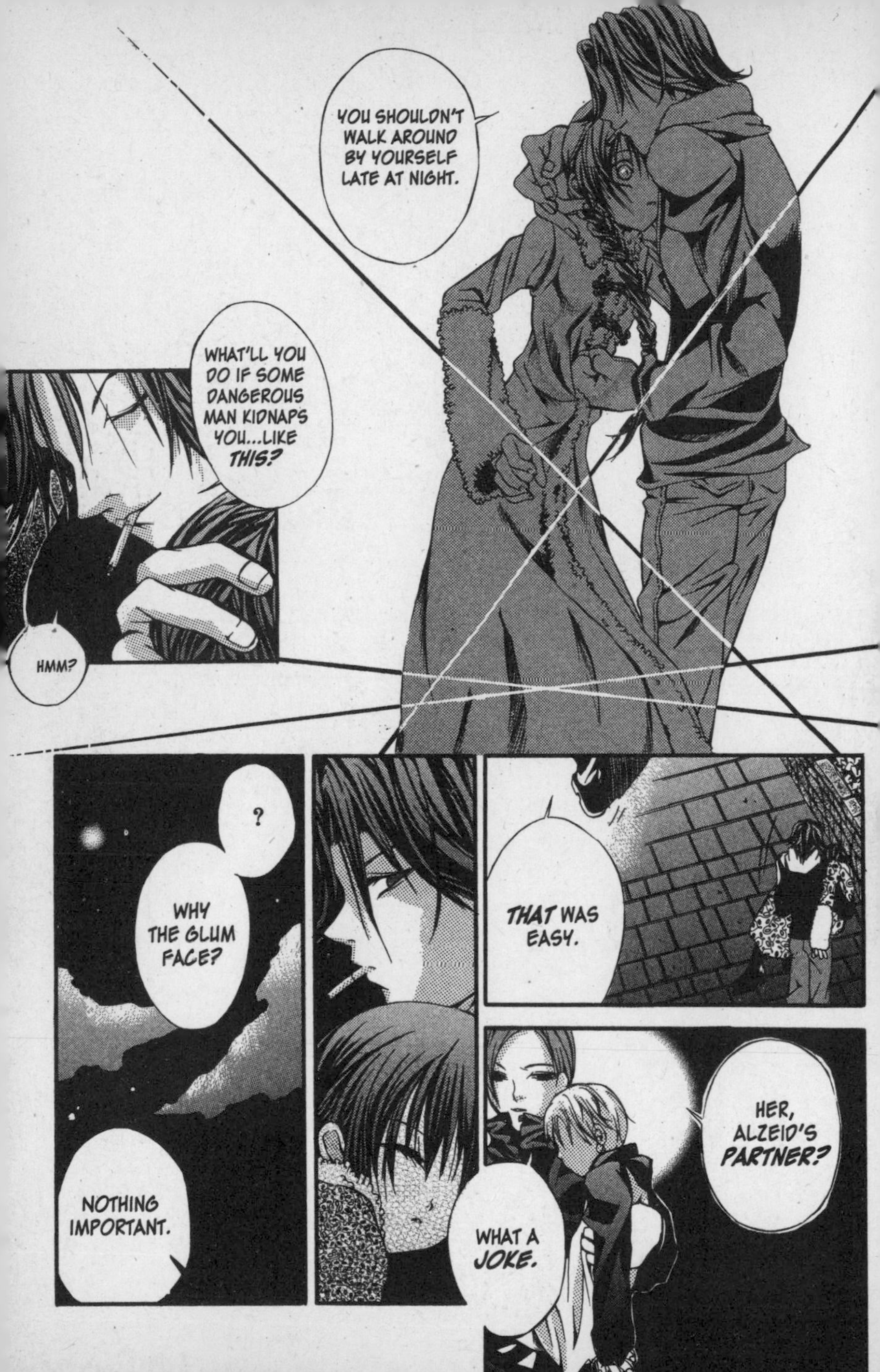
YOU SHOULDN'T WALK AROUND BY YOURSELF LATE AT NIGHT.
WHAT'LL YOU DO IF SOME DANGEROUS MAN KIDNAPS YOU...LIKE *THIS?*
HMM?
THAT WAS EASY.
HER, ALZEID'S *PARTNER?*
WHAT A *JOKE.*
?
WHY THE GLUM FACE?
NOTHING IMPORTANT.

JUST THAT I HOPE DEAR, SWEET RAHZEL WON'T HATE ME FOR THIS.
SHE HATES YOU AL-READY.
I'M VERY EXCITED TO SEE HOW ALZEID WILL REACT! ♡
......
And where was Alzeid then?
He didn't have anything else to do, so he went straight to sleep.

God is watching us

Play our games.

Chapter 9:

Nowhere to Go--Part 4: Broken Wings

WHERE AM I...?

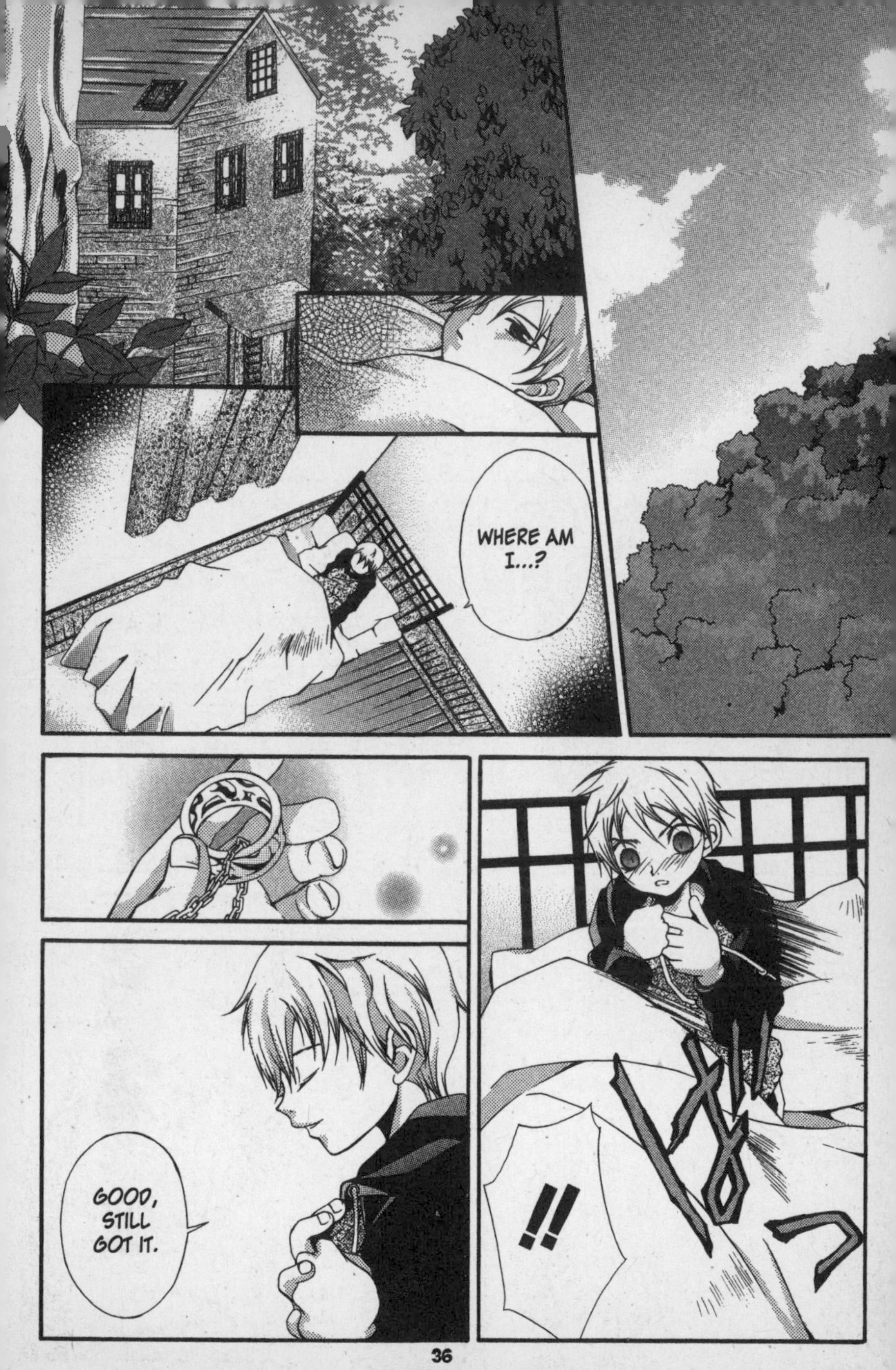

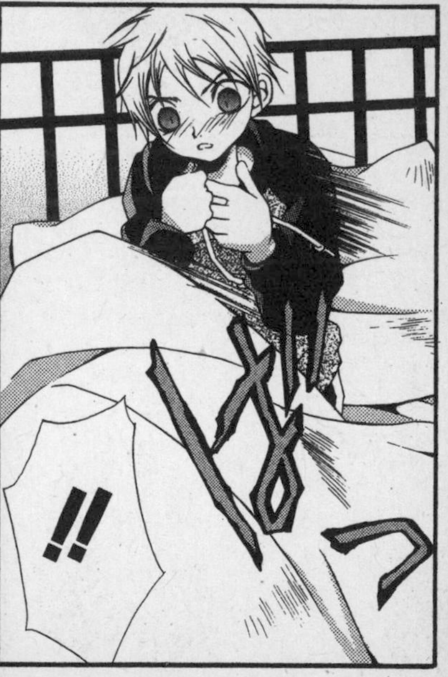
!!

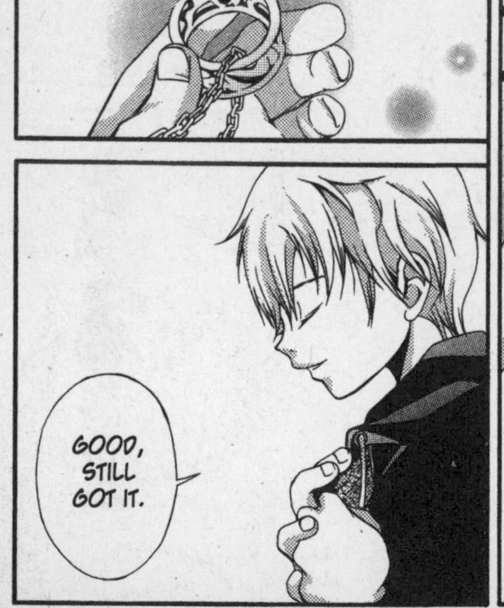
GOOD, STILL GOT IT.

SO STUPID...
THE ONLY THING PROVING THE RELATIONSHIP IS THIS PIECE OF CRAP...
EVERYONE'LL LOVE ME... YOU'RE SUCH A FOOL!
WHO'S A FOOL?
IT'S NONE OF YOUR BUSI-NESS!
DON'T EAVESDROP WHEN I'M TALKING TO MYSELF, OLD MAN!
Old man?!
I SEE. YOU'VE BEEN HIDING YOUR TRUE FACE.
IS THIS THE REAL YOU?
Shocker!
I'VE BEEN ACTING LIKE AN "HONEST AND MOD-EST CHILD" JUST AS YOU WISHED.

I DON'T KNOW WHAT YOU GUYS ARE SCHEMING, BUT IT'S NO USE.
YOU'RE GONNA BE THE ONES CRYING IN THE END.

IF YOU KEEP TALKING LIKE THAT...

...I SHALL HAVE TO HURT RAHZEL IN YOUR PLACE.

BASTARD! RAHZEL HAS NOTHING TO DO WITH THIS!
IN YOUR POSITION, YOU'VE NO RIGHT TO DE-CIDE THINGS LIKE THAT, DO YOU?

SO BE A GOOD BOY AND PLAY ALONG, ALL RIGHT?

DARN IT!
HEY, VEE?
CAN YOU TRUST ME?

ALTHOUGH SHE MUST HAVE DOUBTED ME THEN...

...SHE STILL PROTECTED ME WITHOUT ASKING ANYTHING OF ME!

IT'S MY TURN TO PROTECT HER!

OPEN WIDE! SAY AHHHHH!

AHHHHH...!

I WANTED TO TEACH YOU HOW ADULTS PLAY TOGETHER.
Bzzt! Try doctor and patient.
SO THIS IS COPS AND ROBBERS?
--ARE YOU KIDDING ME? WHY AM I HAND-CUFFED?!
YOU'RE ONE SICK BASTARD!
Hmm?
I ALREADY SENT A MES-SENGER TO ALZEID.
Oww!
SO UNTIL HE COMES TO GET YOU, JUST BE PATIENT.

Heh heh
DON'T BE SURPRISED IF HE DITCHES YOU, THOUGH.

SO YOU GUYS HAVE OTHER PEOPLE WORKING FOR YOU?
IS VEE OKAY?
YOU'RE BETTER OFF WORRYING ABOUT YOUR OWN NECK.
VINCENT IS THE CHILD OF THE KING OF OBPLAY AND HIS MAIDSERVANT.
HE DIDN'T ALWAYS HAVE OFFICIAL RECOGNI-TION.
BUT AFTER ALL THE HEIRS TO THE THRONE SUD-DENLY DIED IN AN EPIDEMIC, THEY DECIDED TO TAKE VEE BACK IN AND MAKE HIM AN HEIR.
THAT RING VEE'S WEARING ON A CHAIN WAS GIVEN TO HIS MOTHER BY THE KING.
IT'S THE PROOF OF HIS IDENTITY.

I DON'T CARE ABOUT THAT.
HOW'D HIS BABY-SITTERS TURN INTO KIDNAPPERS?
WHAT DO YOU WANT? MONEY?
I SAID, I ***HAVE*** KILLED SOMEONE BEFORE! YOU WANNA BE NEXT?!
DON'T MONKEY AROUND WITH ME! I'M GONNA KICK YOUR ASS!
YOU WOULDN UNDERSTAND EVEN IF EXPLAINE IT TO YO
YOU'RE JUST A GIRL WHO'S NEVER KILLED ANYONE.
BUT I HAVE.
BY THE WAY, COULD YOU GET ME DOWN FROM HERE?

You can bathe anytime, if you let me watch you.
When you're in a position like that, you're supposed to call me "Master."
Dammit! Shut your trap!
I'm simply saying I want you to take off these hand-cuffs! Idiot!
UGH! SHE'S LIKE A WILD MONKEY!
WHY IN THE WORLD WOULD ALZEID...
...WANT TO TRAVEL WITH SUCH A KID?
I GUESS IT'S BECAUSE SHE'S A WOMAN?
I DON'T THINK ALZEID'S GAY.
WE'RE PARTNERS.
AT LEAST FOR THE TIME BEING.
IF YOU THINK THE ONLY KIND OF RELATION-SHIP THAT CAN EXIST BETWEEN A MAN AND A WOMAN IS ONE OF LOVE...
...YOU MUST BE SEXUALLY FRUS-TRATED.

Slam
OH NO... YOU CUT YOUR LIP.
Lemme see it.
IT'S FINE.

HMM, I MAY HAVE A CHARACTER FLAW.
JUST NOW, I COULDN'T HELP BUT THINK, "I WON!"
It hurts, though.

I THINK IT'S OKAY TO FEEL SUPERIOR SOMETIMES.

ALZEID IS VERY QUIET, SO HE PROBABLY NEVER LETS PEOPLE KNOW WHAT HE'S FEELING...
...BUT I THINK HE ACTUALLY CARES ABOUT YOU AND SORESTA.
I'M SURE THAT YOU GUYS SHARED A LOT OF MEMORIES WITH ALZEID BEFORE I EVEN KNEW HIM.
SO SORESTA HAS NO REASON TO BE JEALOUS OF ME.

AMAZING HOW YOU CAN BE SO SMART AND SO STUPID AT THE SAME TIME.
HUH?
YOU'RE A SOFTY. YOU'RE GENEROUS TO A FAULT.

SO I THINK I'LL DIVEST YOU OF ***THIS!*** ♪
EEEEK!!

Are you trying to be a sexy fighter like Fujiko in Lupin the Third?
YOU'RE NOT PLANNING TO WAIT FOR ALZEID TO RESCUE YOU, ARE YOU?

Slam

WELL, WELL...
...SINCE YOU EXPECT ME TO, I GUESS NOW I *HAVE* TO ESCAPE BY MYSELF.

DARN IT!
IF I COULD USE MY MAGICAL POWER, I WOULDN'T HAVE TO DO IT LIKE THIS...

!!

OWW!!

HEH HEH...
I GUESS THAT HAND WON'T BE WORKING WELL FOR A WHILE.

WHEN FRISKING A CAPTIVE, IT'S IMPORTANT TO BE THOROUGH.
hoip

キィ
VEE?

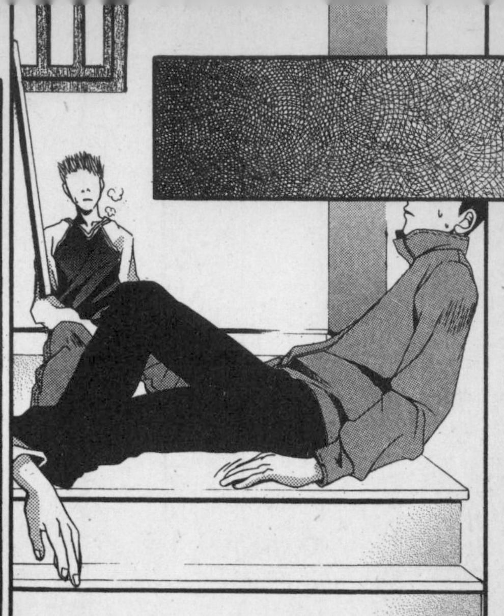

Dammit!
HE'S NOT HERE, EITHER.

NO CHOICE. I HAVE TO GO BACK TO THE FIRST FLOOR AGAIN...
WAAAAHH!!

DAMMIT!
LET ME GO, JERK!
UGH! HOLD STILL!
YO!
RAHZEL!!
Yay!
Squash!

I'M GLAD YOU'RE ALL RIGHT!
THAT'S ENOUGH, KIDS!
HE'S MY HOSTAGE. ♡
PLEASE THROW DOWN YOUR WEAPON, RAHZEL.

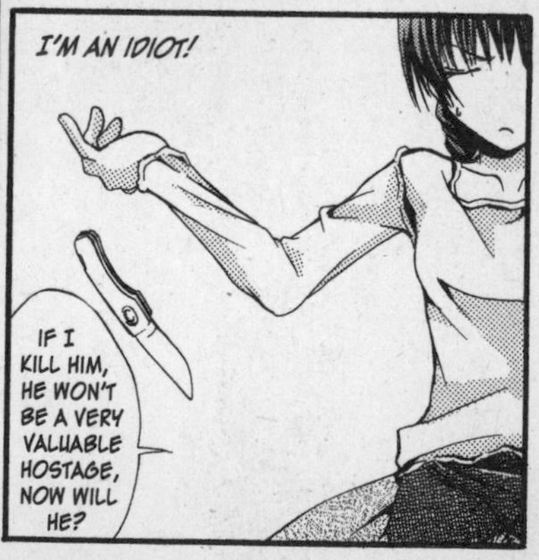

THAT SURPRISES ME--I THOUGHT YOU WERE SCARED TO DO THINGS ALONE.
THAT'S MY BOY!
THAT WAS PRETTY BRAVE, VEE.
Who cares?! Jus hurry and get off me!
YEAH...
I THINK YOU'RE PRETTY BRAVE TO ESCAPE LIKE THAT TOO, RAHZEL.
YOU MUST BE IN PAIN.
I never thought you were going to make a boy cry.
PLUS, IT'S HARD TO FIGHT IN A LONG SKIRT.
IT'S JUST ANOTHER HANDICAP.
BUT EVEN IF I HAD MORE FLEXIBLE CLOTHES ON AND I COULD USE MY MAGICAL POWER...
...AND I CHEATED A LITTLE BIT...
...I KNOW I STILL COULDN'T DEFEAT YOU.

DID YOU DISLOCATE YOUR WRIST?
I DON'T UNDER-STAND WHY YOU'D HURT YOURSELF TO ESCAPE.
THE PRINCESS IS JUST SUPPOSED TO WAIT FOR THE PRINCE TO COME RESCUE HER.

......
YOUR HAND...

NAH. WEARING GLASS SLIPPERS AND BEING AWAKENED BY A KISS JUST ISN'T MY STYLE.
LISTEN UP!
THERE'S THIS WONDERFUL ANCIENT CHINESE SAYING...

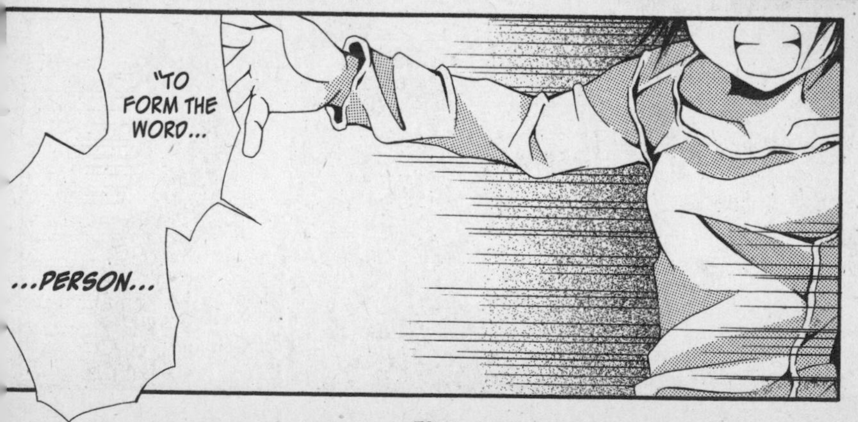
"TO FORM THE WORD...
...PERSON...

The Chinese character for "person."
人
...OBVIOUSLY THE LINE ON THE LEFT IS RELYING ON THE LINE ON THE RIGHT!"
Hmph!

UMM, ISN'T THAT SUPPOSED TO BE "BOTH LINES HAVE TO SUP-PORT EACH OTHER"?
IF ***THAT*** WERE TRUE, IT WOULDN'T BE FAIR FOR ONE TO BE SHORTER THAN THE OTHER!
BY THE WAY, IF YOU FLIP IT AROUND SO THE RIGHT LINE'S LEANING ON THE LEFT LINE, IT MEANS "ENTER."
I've drawn it so you can understand.

SINCE PEOPLE CAN'T SUPPORT EACH OTHER UNLESS THEY'RE ALL AT THE SAME LEVEL...

ANYWAY, MY HAND HURTS, AND I'M ALSO A BIT SCARED... BUT I'VE GOT NO OTHER CHOICE.

...I'LL DO MY BEST TO CLIMB UP AS HIGH AS I CAN!

SO I'M GOING TO CHALLENGE MYSELF TO DO MORE CRAZY THINGS AND BECOME MORE STUBBORN!

THE GUY I'M TRAINING WITH ISN'T EXACTLY ***NORMAL,*** YOU KNOW?

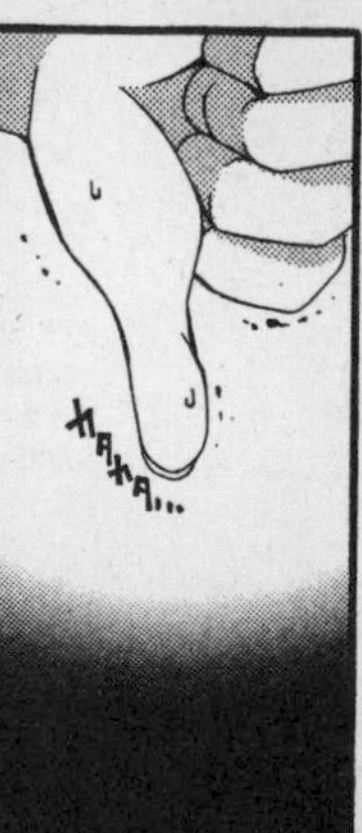

I TAKE IT YOU'RE NOT GOING TO BEG FOR YOUR LIFE?

WHEN I DIE, I PLAN TO BE LAUGHING HYSTERI-CALLY!

WELL, YOU'VE CON-VINCED ME! FROM NOW ON, I'M ON *YOUR* SIDE!
WHAT THE HELL?!

ぱちくり。
?
??

YOU'VE GOTTA BE KIDDING, BAROQUEHEAT!
NOPE. I JUST REALIZED I CAN'T HAVE NEAR AS MUCH FUN WITH A CORPSE.
IF YOU WANT TO BLAME ANYTHING, BLAME YOUR OWN GENDER. ♡

YOU'D BETTER HIGH-TAIL IT WITH THAT KID BEFORE IT GETS MESSY, RAHZEL.
I'LL FOLLOW YOU AS SOON AS I CAN. NOW GET.
ぼーぜん
つんっ
......
How come you're so stiff?
ARE YOU PLANNING TO TAKE US ALL ON BY YOUR-SELF?!
WOULDN'T IT BE NICER FOR YOU TO JUST STAND THERE WAVING FAREWELL TO US WITH HANDKER-CHIEFS?
FINE, THEN. LET'S FIGHT!
BUT I GOTTA WARN YOU, I'M PRETTY GOOD AT IT.
AND I'M NOT GONNA SHOW ANY MERCY--EVEN IF YOU GET ON YOUR KNEES AND BEG, GOT IT?
YOU GOTTA BE KIDDING!

YOU TALK PRETTY BIG FOR SOMEONE IN YOUR SITUATION.

HOW YOU GONNA FIGHT WITHOUT A SWORD?

YOU'RE DEAD MEAT!

HA HA...
NO SWORD?

WHAT DOES *THIS* LOOK LIKE?

COME ON, BOYS!
I'M GOING TO MAKE YOU FEEL SO GOOD...
...THAT YOUR SYNAPSES WILL SHORT OUT!

*Note: See vol. 1, chapter 4.

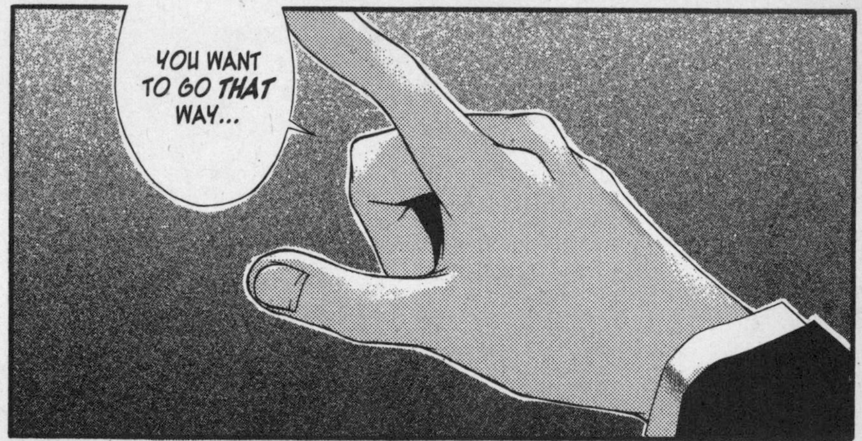

YOU'D BETTER HURRY...
...OR YOU'LL SEE A LOT OF BLOOD-SHED.

WHO ARE YOU?
AND WHAT'S THIS ABOUT BLOOD-SHED?
AAH, WHO AM I INDEED?
FRIEND, OR FOE?
QUIT FOOLING AROUND!
WHO I AM ISN'T IMPOR-TANT.
WHAT MATTERS MOST FOR YOU RIGHT NOW IS GET-TING TO YOUR *PRECIOUS* FRIEND.
ISN'T THAT RIGHT?

I'VE BEEN EXPECTING YOU, ALZEID.

AS YOU KNOW, THE GIRL'S A REAL SHREW.

I FIGURE SHE'S GIVEN YOU ENOUGH TROUBLE BY NOW.

I'M KIND OF IN A BAD MOOD...
...SINCE I DIDN'T EAT BREAKFAST YET.
I'll finally go eat after this.
FOR THAT REASON...
...I WANNA GET THIS OVER AS QUICKLY AS POSSIBLE.
YOU'RE SO SIMPLE.
I'VE ALWAYS LOVED THAT ABOUT YOU.
AND NOW...
...TO THE DEATH.

Chapter 10: Nowhere to Go--Part 5: Quiet Rain

Equipment furnished.
WHAT'S THE PRIZE FOR WINNING?
THE PRINCESS.
THAT'S THE WAY IT ALWAYS IS.
LET ME EXPLAIN THE RULES...
YOU WIN WHEN YOU DEFEAT ALL THE MEN HERE.
BUT IF YOU USE MAGIC, YOU LOSE AUTOMATI-CALLY.
HA!
WHAT A FABULOUS PRIZE.
OH DEAR... I DIDN'T SAY "START" YET.

IT'S BEEN A LONG TIME SINCE I LAST HELD A SWORD.
LET ME PRACTICE A BIT.
NOW IT'S A ONE-ON-ONE FIGHT.
IN THAT CASE, I'LL EVEN THE ODDS.
YOU'RE PRETTY CRUEL. WEREN'T THEY YOUR FRIENDS?
I CAN'T BELIEVE I'M HEARING THOSE WORDS COME OUT OF YOUR MOUTH.
YOU WEREN'T ALWAYS SO SWEET.
......

FIGHTING YOU LIKE THIS SURE TAKES ME BACK TO THE FIRST TIME WE MET.
I HEARD SOMEONE BET HIS LIFE I'D WIN THAT FIGHT...
SO THAT MADE ME WANT TO MEET HIM...BUT THE WAY YOU REACTED...
WHAT ARE YOU TALKING ABOUT?
WHAT DO YOU WANT?
I JUST WANT...
I DON'T REMEMBER THAT AT ALL.
THAT'S EXACTLY HOW IT HAPPENED!

TELL ME, ALZEID...
HOW COME YOU JUST LEFT WITHOUT SAYING GOODBYE?
WE DIDN'T HAVE A CHANCE TO FIGHT MUCH, SINCE THAT LITTLE CIVIL WAR DIDN'T LAST VERY LONG.
BUT MY LIFE WITH YOU AND BAROQUE-HEAT WAS SO HAPPY.
AND WHEN THE WAR ENDED AND YOU BOTH QUIT THE ARMY...I LOST *EVERY-THING.*

VINCENT IS MY TICKET TO GET EVERYTHING BACK.
Where are we now?!
I think it's this way.
USING HIM, I COULD STAGE A COUP D'ETAT OR START A WAR...

THE SWEET SMELL OF BLOOD, THE FEEL OF SLASHING MUSCLE AND BONE...
THE MERE THOUGHT MAKES ME TREMBLE ALL OVER.
THE BATTLEFIELD IS THE ONLY PLACE I AM TRULY *ALIVE*.

I WANT TO GO BACK THERE...

...WITH YOU.

YOU SOUND LIKE A *PERVERT*.

URK!!
I'M SORRY TO DISAPPOINT YOU. BATTLE-FIELDS DON'T INTEREST ME ONE BIT.
KILLING STRANG-ERS...
...GIVES ME NEITHER PAIN NOR SATISFAC-TION.
SORESTA ...
THE SAME GOES FOR KILLING *YOU.*

ANY LAST WORDS?
NONE.
RAHZEL'S HIS PARTNER, AND I'M JUST A STRANGER TO HIM.
I SEE.
SO LONG, THEN.

GREETINGS, KIND SIR!
CARE TO JOIN ME FOR A CUP OF TEA?

WHAT KIND OF ENTRANCE WAS *THAT?*

BY THE WAY, I'M FLIPPIN' COLD, SO GIMME YOUR JACKET!
AND I'VE GOT A DISLOCATED JOINT I WANT YOU TO FIX.
NO THANKS.
I wrapped my hand up good! See?!
YO, WHAT'S UP, SORESTA?

WHAT'S GOING ON? DID YOU... BETRAY ME?
Hey! Be gentle!
I'M ROUGH WITH GIRLS ONLY IN BED. ♡
Though places other than bed can be just as fun. ♡

WELL, SEE YA 'ROUND!
BA-ROQUE-HEAT...

RAHZEL! YOU FORGOT YOUR COAT!

PLEASE ACCEPT IT WITH ALL MY LOVE!

EW! I'D RATHER GET A ***NEW*** ONE! BUZZ OFF!

NO WAY...

THAT'S WHERE I USED TO BELONG.

PLEASE DON'T HATE ME. I'LL BUY YOU DINNER.

He doesn't get what they're talking about. →

WITH DESSERT ...?

WITH DESSERT! ♡

And no smoking, promise?

......

THAT'S WHERE I SHOULD BELONG.

AND I CAN AGAIN...

...ONLY IF YOU ARE GONE!!

I JUST WANT...
...TO BE YOUR FRIEND.
OR IF YOU DON'T WANT TO BE FRIENDS, I CAN TAKE OVER YOUR CLEAN-ING DUTIES OR BRING YOU YOUR MEALS...
Rraaagh!!
YOU ASK-ING ME TO TREAT YOU LIKE SOME ERRAND BOY?
YOU'RE WEIRD.

RAHZEL !!
THIS WHOLE TIME...
...WHAT I REALLY WANTED WAS RIGHT WITHIN MY GRASP...

BUT I GUESS NOW...
...IS A LITTLE LATE TO REALIZE THAT...
?
DO YOU GET WHAT I'M TELLING YOU NOW?!
I'M NOT REALLY VINCENT!
MOTHER WAS A VERY KIND PERSON.
SHE TOOK ME IN AND RAISED ME AS HER VERY OWN CHILD.

THEN WHERE'S THE *REAL* VINCENT?
DEAD.

HE DIED SIX MONTHS AGO FROM THE SAME DISEASE AS EVERYONE ELSE IN THE ROYAL FAMILY.
IT'S SUCH A STUPID STORY.

HE KEPT ASKING MOM "WHEN IS MY DAD COMING TO SEE ME?" UNTIL HE DIED.
AND MOM JUST CRIED AND TOLD HIM, "HE'LL BE HERE SOON."
IT'S *SO* CONVENIENT FOR HIS DAD TO WANT TO SEE HIM...
...NOW THAT HE'S LOST ALL HIS OTHER HEIRS.

I WENT ALONG WITH THIS JUST BECAUSE I WANTED TO *KICK* HIS *ASS* FOR VEE'S SAKE.
I HAD NO IDEA IT WAS GOING TO BE SUCH A LONG JOURNEY.
THIS BLASTED RAIN...

...BETTER HURRY UP...
...AND STOP.
WHAT THE HELL ARE YOU DOING, STUPID CHICK?

I BROUGHT YOU AN UMBRELLA BECAUSE IT'S RAINING.
THEN HOW COME YOU WERE HIDING?

IT LOOKED LIKE YOU WERE CRYING...

NOW LOOK WHAT YOU DID! THE RAIN GOT *WORSE* BECAUSE YOU SAID SOME-THING *STUPID!*
Bash!
SHUT UP, RAIN MAN!
WAAAH! SO COLD!

WHY'D YOU HAVE TO GO AND BREAK THE UMBREL-LA?!
AH HA HA! YOU'RE SOAKING WET!
WHAT'S SO FUNNY ABOUT THAT?!

I CAN'T EVEN SAY "I'M SORRY" OR "THANK YOU."

WHAT AM I SAYING? THIS IS SO EMBARRASSING.

AND NOW I'M WET ALL THE WAY TO MY UNDERWEAR.

IT FEELS PRETTY GROSS.

ALL I CAN DO IS TO WATCH HIM FROM FAR AWAY.

I'M POWERLESS.

I AM SO...
WE'RE GONNA CATCH COLDS.
LET'S HURRY BACK.
...POWER-LESS.
ARE YOU CRYING?
IT'S THE *RAIN*, OF COURSE!
DO YOU NEED GLASSES OR SOMETHING?!

ARE YOU REALLY LEAVING NOW?

I THINK IT'S A BAD IDEA FOR YOU TO GO LIVE SOME-ONE ELSE'S LIFE.
I'VE GOTTA FINISH WHAT I STARTED.

WELL, I CAN SEE THE PEOPLE WHO'RE WAIT-ING FOR ME. I'M OFF!
WAIT!

IS THIS FOR REVENGE?!

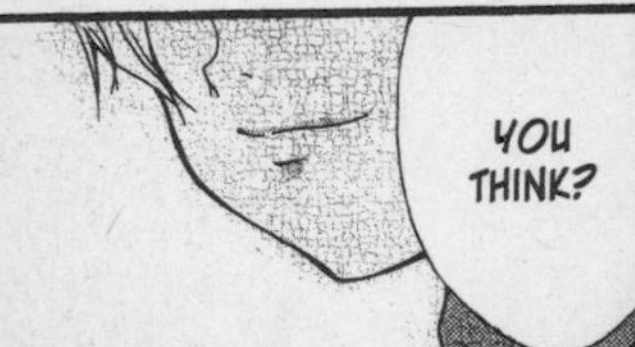
YOU THINK?

NAH. NOW I'M JUST CURIOUS TO SEE WHAT HAPPENS NEXT.

YOU GONNA MISS HIM, RAHZEL?
A LITTLE.
AND I GUESS THIS IS WHERE *WE* SAY GOODBYE AS WELL.

ARE YOU GUYS IGNORING ME?!
HEY, ALZEID! ARE YOU MAD AT ME 'CAUSE I KISSED RAH-ZEL?
YOUR ANGER'S UNDER-STANDABLE, SINCE IT *WAS* HER FIRST KISS.
DEGREE OF HARDNESS = CALCIUM X 2.5 + MAGNESIUM X 4.0.
AT THE FOUNT OF ALL PURITY, IS THERE SOME-ONE WHO TASTES THE WATER?
THERE ISN'T.
AND HOW SWEET AND WONDERFUL IT WAS!
HEY! IF YOU SAY ANOTHER WORD...
...I'M GONNA...
NOW WE *ALL* SHARE THE KISS. ♡

There, there. Don't be scared.
I SOLVED HIS PROBLEM. NOW WE SHOULD *KISS AGAIN...*
click
Wha wha wha...

PREPARE TO MEET YOUR MAKER.

BANG!
WHOOOA! IT WAS JUST A HARMLESS JOKE!
CAREFUL! I'M GONNA DIE! SERI-OUSLY!
BANG!
WHO'S MY MAKER, ANY-WAY?!
I DID NOT JUST SEE THAT...

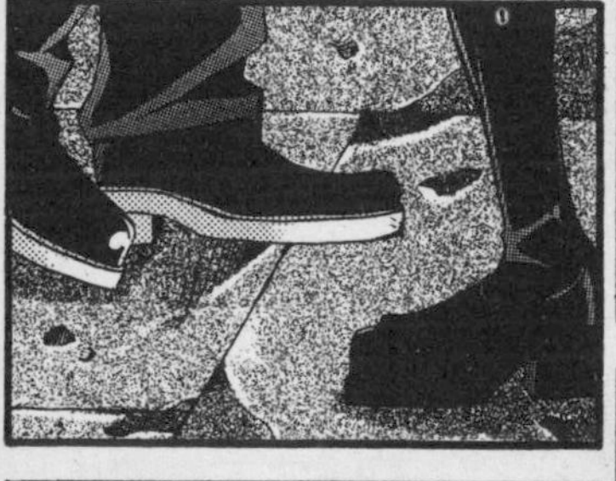

IT'S THAT GUY FROM YESTER-DAY...

THE PIECES HAVE ALL BEEN GATHERED.

SO NOW...
...LET THE GAME BEGIN!
?!

KEEP WALKING!
EH? BUT WHAT ABOUT BAROQUE-HEAT...?
PAY ATTENTION!
SHUT UP!
HE'S GONE?!
FORGET ABOUT THAT KISS. PRETEND YOU JUST GOT LICKED BY A SNAIL.
LIKE I COULD FORGET SOMETHING LIKE THAT!
YOU'RE NOT HELPING AT ALL!

......
Intermission: Morning Scenery
※ Just think of it as the morning of Chapter 8.
こねこね
ぐちゃぐちゃ
Zzz...

RAHZEL, WHAT ARE YOU DOING UP SO EARLY IN THE MORNING?

I'M MAKING A BORIC ACID BALL.

THERE'S A COCKROACH THAT'S BEEN BUGGING ME FOR THE LAST THREE DAYS...

...AND I WANT TO TAKE CARE OF HIM.

How to make a boric acid ball: Mix flour, boric acid and water, knead it and form it into a ball.

:Warning: Extremely toxic to humans.

HERE. TRY SOME! ♡

YOU TRYIN' TO KILL ME?!

WHAT'S THIS? AM I A *COCKROACH* TO YOU?

LET ME EXPLAIN IT GENTLY. YOU'RE A COCKROACH SCHMUCK.

Wow.

I CAN'T BELIEVE HOW MUCH YOU HATE ME.

I WAS THE YOUNGEST CHILD OF FOUR SIBLINGS, AND I ALWAYS WANTED TO BE AN OLDER BROTHER.

SO I WAS GLAD TO HAVE YOU IN MY LIFE LIKE A LITTLE SISTER.

SORRY IF I MADE YOU FEEL BAD, TRYING TO BE SO CLOSE TO YOU.

BAROQUE-HEAT...

WHAT'S *THAT* SUPPOSED TO MEAN?

YOU'D ACTUALLY KISS YOUR *SISTER?*

YOU REALLY ARE ONE SICK BASTARD!

Kill

IT WAS JUST A LITTLE PHYSICAL CONTACT TO SHOW MY AFFECTION! ♡

ANYWAY, HOW *DOES* ALZEID SLEEP THROUGH ALL THIS RACKET?
I TRIED TO WAKE HIM UP, BUT HE WON'T BUDGE. I NEED HIM TO GIVE ME SOME PHYSICAL TRAINING.

PHYSICAL TRAINING? WHY'D YOU WANNA DO SOMETHING LIKE THAT?
Fast asleep.

MY PHYSICAL STRENGTH'S ALL I CAN RELY ON, SINCE I CAN'T USE MY MAGICAL POWER RIGHT NOW.
ONCE I'VE TRAINED ENOUGH...
...IT'LL BE TIME TO BEGIN THE SPECTACULAR "RAHZEL FIGHTING SOUL LEGEND"!

I COULD ALSO CALL IT "THE LEGEND OF BLOODY FRIDAY."
TODAY IS TUESDAY.

SHUT UP! IT'S *FRIDAY* IN MY *HEART!*
Ah ha ha!
WHATEVER YOU SAY. IT'S STILL TUESDAY.

LISTEN! BRUTAL ATTACKS ALWAYS HAPPEN ON FRIDAY, OKAY?!

......

DON'T YOU FEEL SORRY FOR NOT RESPECTING JASON OR THE EXORCIST?

NEVER HEARD OF 'EM.

HEY, I CAN GIVE YOU SOME BETTER PRACTICE THAN LITTLE BOY AL.

I'M A *MASTER* AT HORIZONTAL TECHNIQUES. ♡

......

NOT ON YOUR LIFE!

Krack

STRIKE FROM THE RIGHT.

ぱたんっ
スー……
(Breathing of a sleeping person.)
WHAT A NICE DAY!
HUH. WHO KNEW BORIC ACID BALLS MADE GOOD SPACKLE...?

Chapter 11: Praying Words

...AND WE'LL GET TO THE TOWN BY EVENING IF WE KEEP FOLLOWING THIS ROAD.
WE'LL FIND A PLACE TO STAY THERE FOR THE NIGHT...
Map
...AND WE'LL ALSO PICK UP SOME SUPPLIES WE NEED.
How are you, everyone? Rahzel here! Long time no talk!
ANY-WAYS...
...WHY IS HE HERE EATING OUR FOOD?!
WHAT THE HELL? "US" MEANS ONLY YOU AND RAHZEL? AND I'M NOT INCLUDED?!
ALZEID, JUST KEEP IGNORING HIM AND PRETEND HE DOESN'T EXIST.

HUH...I THINK *I'M* GETTING BIGGER! WHAT SHOULD I DO, RAHZEL?!

I'M GONNA SLICE YOU UP!

PLAY AFTER CLEANING UP THIS MESS!

Lethal weapon

DAMMIT...

Even though we've got a weirdo tagging along, we're doing fine.

HOW COME YOU GUYS NEVER RUN OUT OF BREATH?!
I WORK OUT A LOT. ♡
すぱ
YOUR ENERGY LEVEL IS ENVIABLE.
You're both monsters!

GOOD JOB GETTING US LOST RIGHT AFTER WE GOT TO THE MOUNTAINS.
NOW WE GET TO SLEEP OUTSIDE IN THE COLD.
WITHOUT ANY EQUIPMENT?
I'LL FREEZE TO DEATH!

IN THAT CASE, IT HELPS TO TOUCH HUMAN SKIN TO GET WARM.

DO STUPID STUFF LIKE THAT AGAIN AND I'LL BREAK YOU INTO PIECES.
CAN'T YOU JUST GET USED TO ME ALREADY...?

YOU'RE RIGHT. I MIGHT'VE BEEN TOO HARD ON YOU.
YEAH! AND I'M NOT ALZEID!
WHY ARE YOU BRINGING *ME* INTO THIS?

Hmph.
A KISS ON THE FOREHEAD IS JUST LIKE A HAND-SHAKE!
YOU CAN'T TELL ME YOUR DAD DOESN'T KISS YOUR FOREHEAD.

I DIDN'T MEAN ANY HARM...
I WAS JUST ENJOYING FINDING OUT THE WEAKNESS OF THE PER-SON I HATE MOST...
...WASN'T I?
UMM ...

......
HOW COULD YOU SAY IT WAS JUST A KISS...?

!!
bonk

?

OUUUCH!!
GOOD! YOU FINALLY MADE ME LAUGH!
And what are you laughing at?!
SINCE WHEN HAVE YOU BECOME SUCH A CRUEL COMEDIAN CHARACTER?!
SINCE YOU'VE STILL GOT SO MUCH ENERGY, USE IT TO GO GET SOME FIREWOOD.
YOU DON'T WANT TO FREEZE TO DEATH, DO YOU?

I GUESS YOU'RE RIGHT.
SO I'M GONNA RUN AROUND AND COLLECT SOME FIREWOOD!
OH MY GOD... SHE'S RUN-NING LIKE A MANIAC!
Yeah!
SHE'S A TRUE IDIOT.
SHE'S SO PURE AND CUTE, ISN'T SHE?
SHE MUST BE EXHAUSTED...
...TRYING TO KEEP UP WITH US AND OUR LONG LEGS.
Hey! This isn't olive oil! It's grape seed oil!
Assistant
So? They're both oil.
And you have to crush the basil by hand!
YET SHE DOES THE SHOPPING, COOKING, AND CLEANING ALL BY HERSELF...
...TO TRY TO PROVE THAT THERE'S SOME WAY SHE CAN BE USEFUL.
SHE FEELS GUILTY THAT SORESTA DIED BECAUSE OF HER.

ARE YOU BLAMING ME?
NOT REALLY. I THINK IT WAS HIS FAULT... PLUS, I'M ON RAHZEL'S SIDE, ANYWAYS.
BUT I WOULDN'T HAVE KILLED HIM.
WERE YOU SO DESPERATE TO RESCUE RAHZEL THAT YOU COULDN'T CONTROL THE STRENGTH OF YOUR POWER?
OR WAS IT THAT YOU COULDN'T FORGIVE SORESTA FOR TRYING TO HARM HER?
OR WHAT? MAYBE YOU'VE FINALLY FLIPPED YOUR LID?

OH DEAR. HAVE I UPSET YOU?
I'M SOO SORRY... ♡
DO YOU LIKE TO PLAY RUSSIAN ROULETTE...
...WITH A FULL CHAMBER?
I'M REALLY SORRY!
WELL, NOW...
WHERE AM I?!
I'm feeling fine.
IF A GIRL GETS A LITTLE LOST, DOES THAT MAKE HER A LITTLE LOST GIRL?
SOMEONE, PLEASE TALK BACK TO ME...
I need a straight man for my jokes.
OH NO...I CAN'T EVEN THINK OF ANY FUNNY JOKES LIKE USUAL.
WELL, ANYWAY, I'D BETTER GATHER SOME FIREWOOD!
I'm feeling fine, but other than that...
...nothing else really seems to be working out for me.

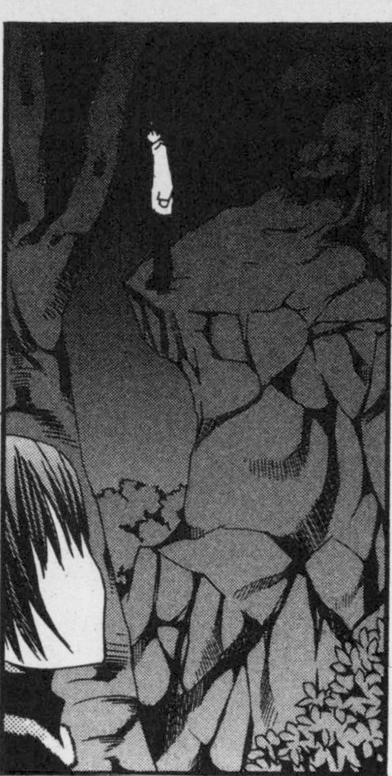

WHAT'S THAT GUY DOING IN SUCH A DANGEROUS PLACE?

I WONDER IF HE'S TRY-ING TO CON-TACT ALIENS? OR MAYBE HE WANTS TO COMMIT SUICIDE?

WELL, IT'S NONE OF MY BUSINESS...
Not my problem.

HEY! YOU TRYING TO KILL YOUR-SELF?!
IF I HAVE TO WATCH YOU DIE, I DOUBT I'LL BE ABLE TO SLEEP FOR THREE WHOLE DAYS!
Eek!
SO PLEASE DO IT SOME-WHERE ELSE!
WHAT ARE YOU TALKING ABOUT?!

I'M AFRAID YOU MIS-UNDER-STOOD.
I WAS JUST TAKING A WALK.

IN A PLACE LIKE THIS?
I LIVE IN A SMALL HOUSE I BUILT NEAR HERE.
YOU MAY THINK ME A BIT ODD, BUT I LIKE THIS PLACE.

NO HARD FEELINGS.

IT'S MY FAULT YOU GOT THE WRONG IMPRESSION.

I'M SORRY. YOU JUST LOOKED SO UNHAPPY FOR SOME REASON.

HERE. I MADE SOME HOT CHOCOLATE.

IT'LL WARM YOU UP.

IF YOU GO OUT THERE IN THE DARK, YOU'LL JUST GET LOST AGAIN. YOU'RE WELCOME TO STAY HERE TONIGHT.

WHY DON'T YOU TRY AND CATCH UP WITH YOUR FRIENDS IN THE MORNING?

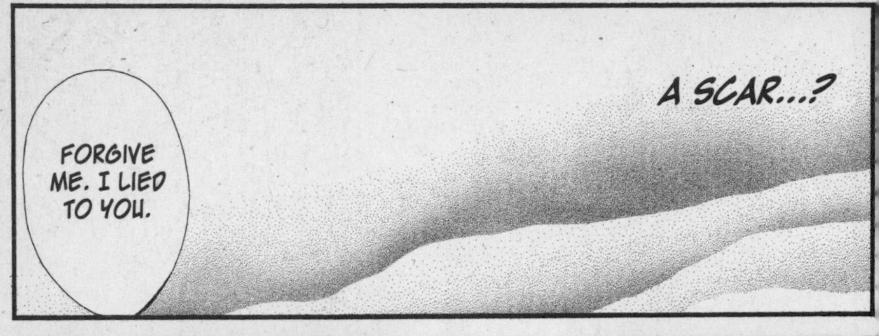
A SCAR...?
FORGIVE ME. I LIED TO YOU.

I JUST COULDN'T DIE.
I'VE TRIED SO MANY TIMES, BUT I JUST CAN'T GO ALL THE WAY.
SO I JUST WANDER AROUND OUT THERE.

WOULD YOU MIND LISTENING TO MY STORY FOR A WHILE?

♪
GOOD MORNING!
WE'VE COME TO COLLECT OUR LOST KITTEN!

Creak

OH! YOU MUST BE HER FRIENDS.
BUT THERE'S NO NEED TO LOOK SO INTIMI-DATING...
Your face is too scary for him.
I was born with this face!

SHE SHOULD BE RESTING FOR A WHILE.
I SHOULD SAY... THAT'S MORE LIKE AN ORDER.
SHE WAS SHOWING SIGNS OF EXHAUSTION.

SHE'S FATIGUED AND HAS A FEVER.

IF *I* WERE HER FRIEND, I WOULDN'T LET HER PUSH HERSELF SO HARD.

PLEASE DON'T MISUNDER-STAND...I'M NOT TRYING TO ASSIGN BLAME.

I USED TO BE A DOCTOR.

THAT IS... UNTIL I KILLED MY WIFE BY MAKING A MISTAKE DURING SURGERY.

THAT WAS SUCH A SHOCK, I HAD TO GIVE UP MY PRACTICE.

I MOVED DEEP INTO THE MOUNTAINS... WHERE I TRIED TO KILL MYSELF BY SLITTING MY WRISTS, AS WELL AS TAKING LOTS OF SLEEPING PILLS...

BUT RAHZEL TOLD ME...

I THINK YOU'VE GOT NO CHOICE BUT TO SUFFER MORE.

......
YEAH, I KNOW. SHE CAN BE BLUNT TO THE POINT OF CRUELTY.
IT WAS YOUR JOB TO SAVE PEOPLE'S LIVES.
YOU WEREN'T ALLOWED TO MAKE MISTAKES.
BUT NOBODY'S PERFECT, AND WE ALL MAKE MISTAKES AT SOME POINT IN OUR LIVES, NO MATTER HOW HARD WE TRY.
BUT EVERY TIME WE DO MAKE A MISTAKE, WE HAVE TO LEARN FROM IT.
I RESPECT YOU FOR SUFFERING...
...AFTER CHOOSING SUCH A BURDENSOME PATH.
BUT SOMEDAY...
...I WANT YOU TO FORGIVE YOURSELF, IF JUST A LITTLE BIT.

I WAS LONELY.
WHEN I COULDN'T HELP BUT FEEL COLD AND DARK AND ALONE...
...HER SIMPLE WORDS FILLED ME WITH HOPE.

HOW LONG D'YOU NEED TO SLEEP?
WAKE UP, STUPID CHICK!
Phoo!
HEY! YOU SHOULD LET HER SLEEP A LITTLE LONGER.

SHE'S THE ONE WHO WANTED TO PUSH HERSELF SO FAR!
And she takes care of everything perfectly.
SHE INSISTS ON DOING EVERYTHING HERSELF.
BUT...

Ummmm...
WHAT IS IT, DADDY?
I'M STILL SLEEPY...

WAKE UP! I'M NOT YOUR FATHER!
Ah!

Gwah...
I can't believe her!
HER SLEEPING POSTURE SUCKS.
......
Are you really worried about her posture?
BUT...
Heh.
...I KNOW YOU'RE CAPABLE OF GETTING A PUDDING OR PUTTING ON YOUR COAT BY YOURSELF...
...WHEN YOU'RE WORN OUT.
AND YOU CAN ALSO PICK UP SCATTERED BONES, RIGHT?
Don't waste my time.
BONES?!

THANK YOU FOR TAKING CARE OF HER!
His danger sense kicked in, so he picked her up before Alzeid got more irritated.
PLEASE WAIT!

IT'S ALREADY DARK OUTSIDE. PLEASE STAY AT LEAST ONE NIGHT IN MY HOME.
I'M SORRY, BUT I MUST REFUSE.

HER DUTY IS WITH US.

YOU CAN'T HAVE HER JUST BECAUSE YOU TOOK A LIKING TO HER.

Ha ha...
IF YOU BECOME TIRED OF HER, PLEASE LEAVE HER WITH ME.
I SUGGEST YOU LOOK FOR SOME-ONE ELSE.
Bye-bye!

SO, WHAT'RE WE GONNA DO NOW?
I DON'T WANNA SLEEP OUTSIDE ANYMORE.
Whoa!
WHERE AM I?
What's going on?!
OH, YOU'RE AWAKE NOW?
YOU CAN GO BACK TO SLEEP IF YOU WANT. I'M BUFF!
DON'T SPOIL HER.

WHAT'D YOU SAY? I CAN'T BELIEVE MY EARS! ALZEID, THE ROMANTIC!

BAROQUEHEAT, YOU CAN DO WHATEVER YOU WANT WITH HER.

REALLY? YEAH! ♡

EEEK!!

PLEASE TELL ME WHY WE HAVE TO GO THROUGH THE FOREST.
THIS IS A SHORTCUT!

IT WOULD'VE BEEN FASTER TO TAKE THE LONGER WAY AROUND, SINCE WE GET LOST SO EASILY IN THE FOREST.

WE ARE NOT LOST!
I CAN'T TRUST YOU.
SHOW ME THE MAP.
IT'LL BE ALL RIGHT!
WE'LL SEE THE TOWN SOON.
SEE...
EEEEEEK?!
WHY DON'T YOU BELIEVE ME?!
HOW CAN I BELIEVE YOU?!

WOW! YOU'RE PRETTY AGGRESSIVE TODAY! IT'S AN HONOR TO BE HUGGED BY YOU! ♡
THINK YOU CAN HOLD BACK UNTIL BEDTIME?
WHAT ARE YOU DOING, IDIOT?!
YOU GUYS ARE THE IDIOTS!
LOOK AT THAT!!

WHAT THE HELL?!

Chapter 12:
The Sun in the Palm--Part 1: Borderline

OH, ARE YOU TALKING ABOUT THE *SKY BURIAL?*

YOU MEAN THE PLACE WHERE THOSE CORPSES ARE LEFT FOR THE VULTURES?
Ughh!
I KNOW IT SOUNDS QUITE BRUTAL...
...BUT IT'S A VERY COMMON PRACTICE IN THIS AREA.

THIS ROOM HAS NO LOCK, SO IF YOU HAVE ANY VALUABLES...
...PLEASE TAKE THEM WITH YOU... UM... HELLO?
YOU'RE THROWING UP DUST!
HEY, THIS BED'S GOT PRETTY GOOD SPRINGS!
GUYS, YOU MIGHT WANT TO LISTEN TO THE HOTEL OWNER'S EX-PLANATION...

IT'S THE SAME OLD EXPLANATION AT EVERY HOTEL...IT'S GETTING TO BE A REAL DRAG.
BUT YOU ALWAYS MAKE A SCENE, SHOUTING, "WHERE'S THE BATHROOM?!"

OH, LARAWELL. I DIDN'T KNOW YOU WERE THERE.

HERE! SAY HELLO TO OUR GUESTS.
"MY NAME IS LARAWELL.
PLEASED TO MEET YOU!"
W-WEL... COME...

GOOD JOB, LARAWELL!
A DOTING FATHER ?!
DOTING FATHER ?!
DOD-DERING IDIOT?
Hug!

THIS IS MY DAUGHTER, LARAWELL.
SINCE MY WIFE PASSED AWAY, LARAWELL IS MY ONLY FAM-ILY AND HOTEL STAFF.
PLEASE LET HER KNOW IF AND WHEN YOU NEED ANYTHING.

BY THE WAY... HOW COME YOU'RE ALL TRAVELING TOGETHER?

YOU DON'T LOOK RELATED...

YEAH... HOW COME...?

IT'S A SCHOOL TRIP, RIGHT?

YOU GUYS...

You just now remembered?

あっ

Ah!

I REMEMBER NOW!

WE'RE IN SEARCH OF THE PERSON WHO KILLED ALZEID'S FATHER!

WHY DO YOU ALWAYS BLURT THINGS TO STRANGERS WITHOUT THINKING FIRST?!

YOU NEVER KNOW WHERE WE MIGHT FIND A CLUE!

THERE COULD BE SOME HERE!

CAN YOU GIVE ME THE PERSON'S DESCRIPTION?

I'M GLAD YOU ASKED!

ふふんっ

NOW, DON'T LET IT FRIGHTEN YOU!

Just like a spring zephyr.

HE'S A GIANT WHO CAN SPLIT THE CLOUDS...

HIS BODY IS COVERED WITH GREEN STEEL SCALES, AND HIS PUPILS ARE VERTICAL SLITS FLASHING IN THE LIGHT...

UNLIKE HIS HIDEOUS APPEARANCE, HE HAS A BEAUTIFUL VOICE LIKE A SPRING ZEPHYR, AND BREATH THAT SMELLS LIKE HERB TEA...

...WHICH HE USES TO ATTRACT TRAVELERS AND SUCK THEM INTO HIS MAW. HE'S A VERY SCARY MONSTER.

WE GOTTA LOOK FOR A ***MONSTER*** LIKE ***THAT?!***

Count me out!

Ha!

THAT'S ALL JUST MY IMAGINATION, OF COURSE.

IT'S A ***WOMAN***...

...WITH LONG BLACK HAIR...
...AND BLUE EYES...

I'VE NEVER HAD ANY GUESTS HERE FITTING THAT DESCRIPTION.

BUT I'VE HEARD THERE'S A VILLAGE DOWN IN THE SOUTH-WEST THAT HAS PEOPLE WITH THAT HAIR AND EYE COLOR.

IT HAPPENED ABOUT THIR-TEEN YEARS AGO. WHERE WERE YOU BACK THEN?

YOU TALKIN' ABOUT *MOI?!*

I WAS J-JUST... ONE YEAR OLD...

Really?

YOU MUST'VE BEEN QUITE AN AGGRESSIVE TODDLER!

SOUTH-WEST! IT'S SOUTHWEST, BAROQUE-HEAT!
Okay, okay.
IF YOU...

IF YOU FIND THE PERSON, WHAT ARE YOU GOING TO DO?

ARE YOU GOING TO *KILL HER?*

LARA-WELL...?
I'M SORRY I ASKED SUCH A STRANGE QUESTION!
I'LL GO MAKE YOU SOME TEA!
DID WE SAY SOMETHING BAD TO HER?
I THINK SHE WAS JUST SCARED OF ALZEID'S FACE.
I'M VERY SORRY...I DON'T THINK THAT WAS THE REASON.
...
HER MOTHER DIED RIGHT AFTER GIVING BIRTH.
Plus she was scared of Alzeid's face.
SHE MUST BE SENSITIVE ABOUT ISSUES LIKE AVENGING A PARENT.
I REGRET THAT SHE HAS TO FEEL INSECURE ABOUT NOT HAVING A MOTHER.
I FEEL BAD FOR HER...
...BUT I WOULD DO ANYTHING FOR MY DAUGHTER.

WHATEVER IT TAKES TO PROTECT HER...
I WAS SURPRISED TO FIND OUT THAT ALZEID'S FATHER'S KILLER WAS A WOMAN.
I SENSE THAT YOU'VE BEEN HIDING SOME DEEP, DARK SECRET FROM US.
THE WHOLE TIME I'VE KNOWN YOU, YOU'VE NEVER HAD ANY WOMEN AROUND.
SWAK
FORBIDDEN LOVE?
I see!
HOW COME YOU DIDN'T GIVE ME HER DESCRIPTION EARLIER?
THAT WOULD'VE MADE LOOKING FOR HER EASIER.
WHY'RE YOU GUYS SO FRIENDLY WITH EACH OTHER ALL OF A SUDDEN?
WAS THAT DESCRIPTION REALLY DETAILED ENOUGH TO BE HELPFUL?
WELL, THAT COLOR COMBINATION'S PRETTY RARE--I SHOULD KNOW.
Hmm...
SO, WHERE SHE CAME FROM IS NOW OUR KEY, NOW.

SO OUR NEXT DESTINATION IS THE PLACE THE OWNER WAS TALKING ABOUT?
YEAH...
I DON'T WANT TO DO THIS...
I DON'T WANT TO GO.
HOW COME?
IF THERE'S A BUNCH OF PEOPLE AROUND WHO LOOK LIKE ME...
...I WON'T STAND OUT ANYMORE!
THINK IT'D BE FASTER TO GO NORTH FIRST AND TAKE A BOAT FROM THERE?
YEAH, SEEMS THAT WAY.
HAVE YOU NO CONSIDERATION FOR MY FEELINGS?!

OF COURSE I'M GONNA IGNORE YOUR STUPID REASON! ARE YOU INSANE?!
I SAID NO!
IT IS A BASIC INSTINCT TO WISH TO BE BETTER THAN OTHERS! I DESERVE TO DEMAND SUCH A WISH!
Knock knock
EXCUSE ME...

ARE WE MAKING TOO MUCH NOISE?
OH, NO.

I WAS WONDERING IF MY DAUGH-TER WAS HERE...
I HAVEN'T BEEN ABLE TO FIND HER.
THEN...
...WHY...

WHY DO WE HAVE TO LOOK FOR HER?
SHUT UP! HELPING PEOPLE IS GOOD!
HEY! LARA-WELL!
RRGH, YOU! SHE'S NOT GONNA BE IN A TRASH CAN!

DO YOU KNOW THE PROVERB "THE BITER IS SOMETIMES BITTEN"?
YOU MAY DISAPPEAR AFTER A FEW HOURS, YOU KNOW.
Put on this nametag right now.
Rahzel
I DON'T KNOW WHAT YOU'RE TALKING ABOUT.

LISTEN... IF THAT LITTLE GIRL IS WALKING AROUND ALONE ON A NIGHT LIKE THIS...
I FOUND A LITTLE GIRL RIGHT HERE!

She's singing the theme song to Karaoke Fighter Virgeman.

I'M GOING TO LOOK FOR HER THIS WAY. YOU GUYS GO LOOK THAT WAY!

♫ Funny Fabulous Karaoke Fighter Virgeman!
♫ Love that yellow uniform! ♪
Protecting the future of the earth! ♪ ♫ ♫
THERE SHE GOES... SHOULD WE START LOOKING SERIOUSLY NOW?
NAH... I'M GOING BACK TO THE HOTEL.

Sleep NOW!

I'M DEAD TIRED.

--WHO *DARES* INSULT ME LIKE THAT?!

?!

GOOD EVENING! ♡

Chapter 13: The Sun in the Palm--Part 2: Where Souls Rest

GOOD EVENING! ♡
WHAT ARE YOU DOING HERE?!
WHO ARE...
!!
WAIT A MINUTE! IF I ASK HIM SUCH A SIMPLE QUESTION...
WHO I AM DOESN'T MATTER!
IDIOT!
...HE'LL JUST GIVE ME AN ANNOYING ANSWER LIKE THAT!

JUST NOW, I DIDN'T SEE ANYONE AT ALL!!
(Trying to convince self.)
Yeah!
YOU CAN'T AVOID REALITY.

WHY ARE YOU WAN-DERING AROUND AT THIS HOUR?
ARE YOU LOOKING FOR A DATE?
I'M LOOKING FOR SOME-ONE.
Don't follow me!

WHAT KIND OF PERSON?

ARE YOU GOING TO HELP ME?!
NO WAY!
ARE YOU STUPID?! I WAS JUST SAYING THAT OUT OF COURTESY.

FIRST I'LL KICK HIS LIVER...
THEN I'LL BREAK HIS ELBOWS...
Mumble...
OH, ACTUALLY, I SAW A LITTLE GIRL WALKING AROUND EARLIER...
...ALTHOUGH I DON'T KNOW IF THAT MIGHT BE WHO YOU'RE LOOKING FOR.

REALLY? WHERE?!
THERE'S A CEMETERY AT THE EDGE OF TOWN.
IT'S A NICE, QUIET PLACE.
I LIKE PLACES WHERE THERE'S NO ONE AROUND.
WHY WERE YOU IN SUCH A CREEPY PLACE?
ARE YOU TALKING ABOUT THE SKY BURIAL THING?
WHAT YOU'RE DOING RIGHT NOW DOESN'T MAKE MUCH SENSE.
WHY ARE YOU RUNNING AROUND LOOKING FOR A STRANGER?
WHEN IT COMES TO YOUR ONE FRIEND AND THAT GIRL...
...YOU ARE MORE LIKE AN IDIOT THAN A HYPOCRITE.
OR COULD YOU JUST NOT SAY NO...
...WHEN YOU WERE PUT ON THE SPOT?
OR WAS IT BE-CAUSE...
...YOU HAVE THE SAME SCAR RIGHT HERE?

HI-YA!!
?!

OUCH!
WHY'D YOU PUNCH ME? YOU'RE SO VIOLENT!
TOUCHING A GIRL'S CHEST IS...
...THE ILLEGAL BEHAVIOR OF A PERVERT!
Don't think you can touch me so easily!

I DIDN'T TOUCH YOUR CHEST.
YOU SURE DID!
BUT, UM...
SHUT THE HELL UP!

……

I AM SORRY.
こくん
ME, TOO.
……

ANYWAYS, I'LL GO LOOK FOR HER THERE.
THANKS A LOT.
YOU'RE WELCOME.

BUT RE-MEMBER...
...WHEREVER YOU GO, WE ARE CON-NECTED BY THE SCAR IN YOUR HEART.
THERE'S NO ESCAPING.
YOU ARE MINE.

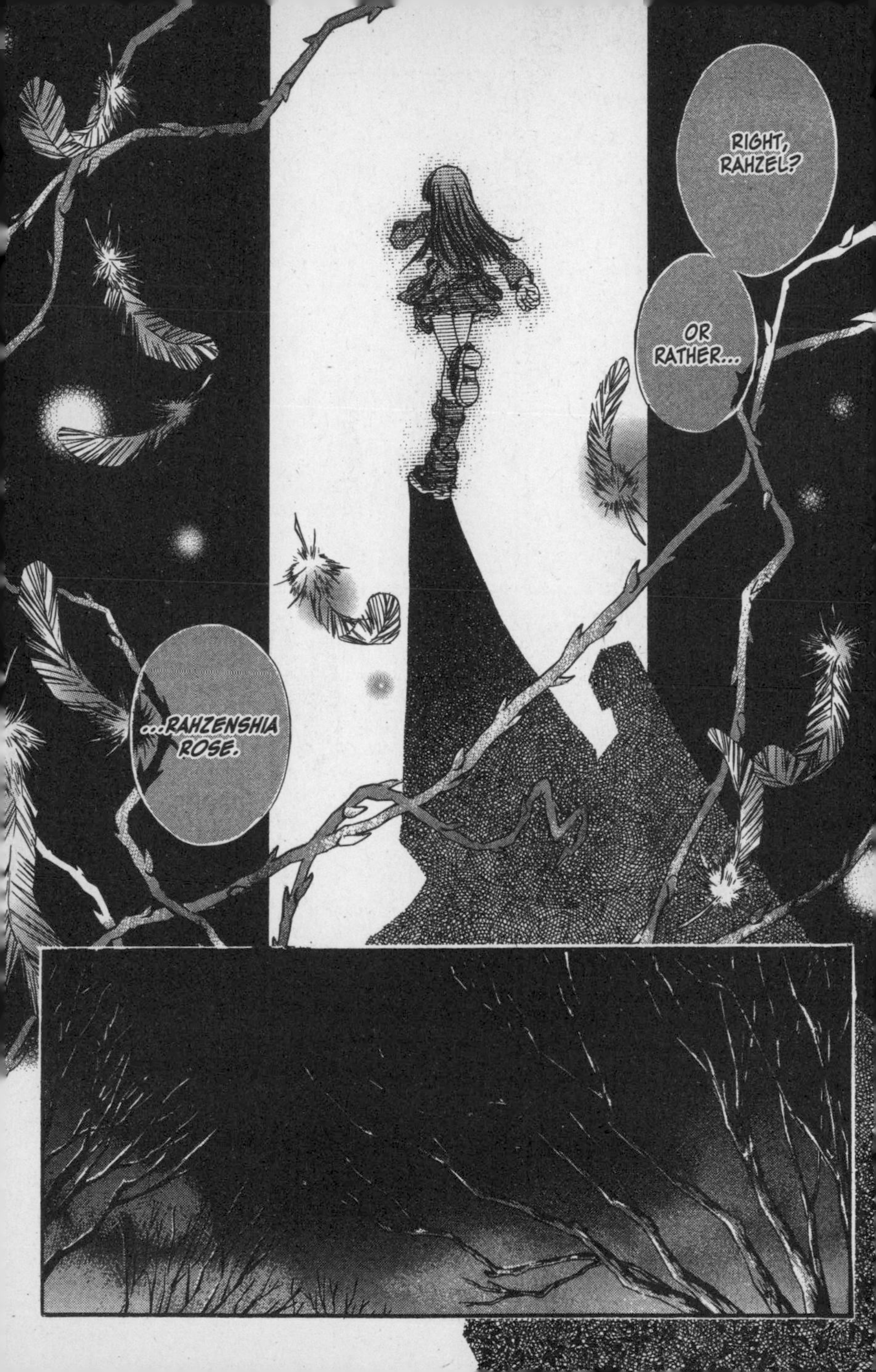
RIGHT, RAHZEL?
OR RATHER...
...RAHZENSHIA ROSE.

FOUND YOU!

YOU'RE VISITING SOMEONE'S GRAVE AT THIS LATE HOUR OF THE NIGHT?
YOU'RE GOING TO CATCH A COLD!

W-WELL...
IT'S RAHZEL.
?
CALL ME RAHZEL.

I DON'T KNOW ABOUT THIS "SKY BURIAL" THING. THERE'S NO HEADSTONE?
ISN'T THAT INCONVEN-IENT?

THAT WAS A LIE...

...THAT SKY BURIAL IS COMMON IN THIS TOWN.

BECOMING THE BLOOD AND FLESH OF THE BIRD...
...EVENTUALLY THEY BECOME THE BIRD ITSELF...
AND THEY CAN FLY FAR AWAY...
ALTHOUGH THAT SOUNDS VERY ROMANTIC...
...A HUMAN BEING HAS MORE ADVANTAGES THAN A BIRD.
ADVANTAGES?
THAT'S RIGHT!!
A HUMAN CAN SURVIVE WITHOUT BEING ABLE TO WALK...
...WHILE A BIRD THAT CAN'T FLY OR A FISH THAT CAN'T SWIM HAS NO CHOICE BUT TO DIE.
WE DEFINITELY HAVE THE ADVANTAGE!
WHY IS THAT SO?
WELL, WHY DO YOU THINK?
IT'LL BE YOUR HOMEWORK UNTIL WE GET BACK TO THE HOTEL.

C'MON!
LET'S GO BACK!

HOW CAN YOU SLEEP SO DEEPLY?!
OH. WEL-COME HOME.
I'M HOME... WAIT! THIS IS NO TIME FOR SUCH A PEACEFUL CONVERSA-TION!
THEN DON'T COME HOME.
WHAT ARE YOU TALKING ABOUT?!
I'M HOME, TOO!

WHY AM I SURROUNDED BY IDIOTS?!
AH HA HA! RAHZEL...ARE YOU THINKING ABOUT SOMETHING NAUGHTY?
WELL... YOU'RE PROBABLY RIGHT.♡

I HATE YOU.
WHERE ARE YOU GOING?!
TO TAKE A SHOWER.

THEN, I'LL WASH YOUR BACK...
GET AWAY FROM ME, PERVERT!

SHE'S IN A BAD MOOD.
Ouch!
IT'S YOUR OWN FAULT, YOU KNOW.
Futon

IT'S ***HER*** FAULT SHE WON'T LET ME DO ANYTHING WITH HER.
I COULD ***FAINT*** FROM SO MUCH FRUSTRATION.
WHAT ARE YOU ASKING FROM THAT CHILD?
I CAN'T GO INTO THE DETAILS, SINCE OUR EDITOR WILL CUT MY LINE.

I'M STRIVING TO BEAR WITH IT AND KEEP MYSELF FROM DOING SOMETHING ILLEGAL...
...BY GETTING SOME EASY ONES HERE AND THERE.
ISN'T THAT NOBLE OF ME?

YOU'RE JUST ASKING ME TO CALL YOU A ROTTEN PERVERT.

WELL, I'M GOING OUT, NOW.
WHERE ARE YOU GOING?
JUST TO CHECK ON OUR PRINCESS' MOOD.

WHAT? DID YOU WANT ME TO TAKE YOU ALONG TO THAT GIRL'S PLACE?

CHOOSE YOUR DEATH. POISONING? STRANGULATION? OR SHOULD I JUST PULL THE TRIGGER?
HLEE HOM HLOO HWEE...

Translation: Please don't shoot me...

DON'T WORRY, I'M NOT GOING TO PEEP.
LITTLE BOY. ♡
ARE YOU SO EAGER TO DIE?
NO WAY! BOOOO!
BYE-BYE! POOOO!
IF YOU VALUE YOUR LIFE, DON'T COME BACK.
I BEG YOU.
UM...
DID YOU COME HERE BECAUSE YOU WERE MAD AT YOUR FRIEND?
CLOSE, BUT THAT'S NOT WHY.

Ah!
WHEN I GOT BACK FROM TAKING A SHOWER, HE WAS FAST ASLEEP.
HE SEEMED LIKE HE WAS IN HEAVEN, AND THAT TICKED ME OFF.
SO I DID SOMETHING TO HIM...AND THEN I CAME HERE BECAUSE I WAS SCARED OF HIS RETALIATION.
Hoo hoo hoo! ♥
WHAT IN THE WORLD DID SHE DO TO HIM?
UMM...
HUH?
CAN YOU GIVE ME THE ANSWER TO THE HOMEWORK?
OH, THAT ANSWER WAS...
..."OUR CULTURE DEVELOPS A SUPPORT SYSTEM."
BUT TO TELL YOU THE TRUTH...
...I THINK THAT'S NOT QUITE RIGHT...
...BECAUSE I JUST CAN'T LIVE BY IT.

THEN WHAT IS YOUR TRUE ANSWER?

IT'S A SE-CRET.

IT'S AN ANSWER JUST FOR MYSELF.

THEN...

...COULD YOU ANSWER *MY* QUESTION?

I AM A ***MURDERER.***

DOES THAT MAKE YOU FEEL DISGUST-ED?

......

LISTEN TO THIS...

IT'S SOMETHING I REMEMBER...
...FROM WHEN I WAS SO SMALL...
...THAT I COULDN'T DO ANY-THING BY MYSELF.
......

SO, AFTER HEARING THAT...

...ARE YOU SCARED OF ME?

IT'S A BITTER PILL...

ARE YOU DISGUSTED BY ME?

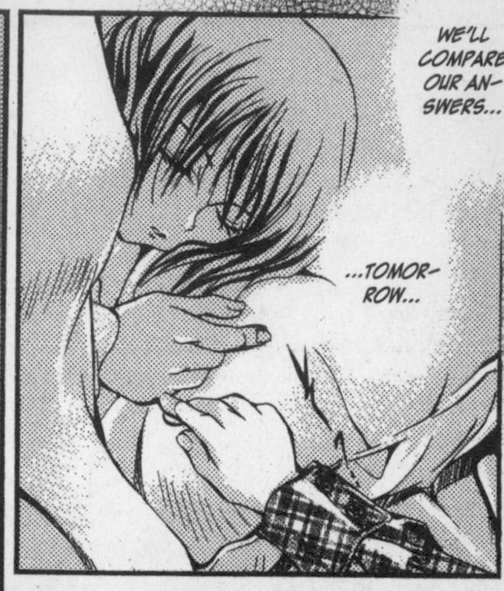
WE'LL COMPARE OUR AN- SWERS...
...TOMOR- ROW...

HEY, ALZEID? CAN I ASK YOU SOME-THING?

JUST SAY IT.

WHAT THE HELL IS UP WITH YOUR HAIR?

Yawn

I HAVE NO IDEA...

GOOD MORNING. YOU GUYS WAKE UP SO EARLY...

YEAH...
DO WE HAVE MATCHING HAIR?
YES! WE DO!
We have different-colored ribbons!
DAMMIT! YOU DID THIS TO ME, STUPID CHICK?!
EEEEK! I'M SORRY!!

Chapter 14: The Sun in the Palm--Part 3: Witch-Hunting

AHH...
...CHOO!!
YOU HAVE A COLD?
Don't spray us.
I GUESS...

Warning: January.

I DON'T FEEL THAT WAY AT ALL.

RAHZEL, WHERE'S THE BUTTER?

?

NOW YOU GET IT?

I SEE NOW WHAT YOU MEAN.

I just felt a chill.

HEY...

I WONDER HOW LARAWELL'S MOTHER DIED...?

LAST NIGHT, I FOUND LARAWELL AT THE SKY BURIAL PLACE.

SHE TOLD ME THAT PLACE IS USED ONLY FOR PEOPLE WHO DIE IN BAD WAYS.

Though that's not how I'd describe it.

I HAVE NO IDEA WHAT YOU'RE TALKING ABOUT.

TRY ORGANIZING YOUR THOUGHTS BEFORE YOU SPEAK.

OH...I'M SORRY.

BUT I BELIEVE THE REASON SHE WAS THERE WAS TO VISIT SOMEONE'S GRAVE. IT MUST BE HER MOM'S.

DYING FROM GIVING BIRTH TO A CHILD...

...DOESN'T SEEM LIKE A *BAD* WAY TO DIE TO ME.

THAT'S A STUPID THING TO SAY. WHAT'S GOOD AND WHAT'S BAD...
...CHANGES IN DIFFERENT CULTURES AND RELIGIONS.
THOUGH I CAN'T UNDERSTAND HOW THEY CAN HAVE SUCH BAD TASTE THAT THEY'D LEAVE A HUMAN BODY TO FEED THE BIRDS.
I CAN'T UNDERSTAND THAT, EITHER.
THEN QUIT WITH THE POINTLESS SPECULATION. JUST GO SHOPPING.
WE'RE LEAVING THIS TOWN TOMORROW.
OH! I GOTTA TALK TO YOU ABOUT THAT.
I DECIDED NOT TO GO TO THAT SOUTHWEST VILLAGE WITH YOU ANYMORE.
WHAT'S GOING ON?
I HAVE NO REASON TO FOLLOW YOU WHEN OUR LOVELY RAHZEL DOESN'T WANT TO GO THERE, EITHER.
By the way, put some clothes on!
HAVE I EVER DONE ANYTHING TO MAKE YOU HAPPY?
NEVER.

IS IT ME?
DO WHATEVER YOU WANT TO DO. I NEVER FORCE ANYONE TO COME WITH ME.
I'LL GO WITH YOU HALFWAY SINCE I FEEL PITY FOR YOU.
BUT AFTER THAT, RAHZEL AND I WILL GO A DIFFERENT DIRECTION.
I'M GLAD.
IS IT MY FAULT THEY'RE IN A BAD MOOD?!
NOW WE'RE GOING TO PREPARE FOR OUR TRIP TOGETHER.
Basically, I'm going on a date with her!
Oh no!
HAVE FUN!
OH NO. YOU REALLY MADE HIM MAD.
I'M GLAD YOU'RE DOING THIS FOR ME, BUT NO FIGHTING, OKAY?
WE FIGHT BECAUSE WE'RE SO CLOSE, Y'KNOW?
It'll be all right.
HEY... BAROQUE-HEAT?
HMM?
YOU WERE EAVESDROPPING ON MY CONVERSATION WITH LARAWELL LAST NIGHT, WEREN'T YOU?
WELL...I WOULDN'T PUT IT THAT WAY.
I WAS INTERESTED IN WHAT'S ON YOUR MIND...
DO YOU WANT TO SAY SOMETHING TO ME?
I'M REALLY SORRY.
BESIDES THAT?

I'M GONNA BUY YOU A MEAT BUN LATER.
GOOD!
I'M ACTUALLY NOT MAD AT ALL...
IT'S NOT LIKE I WAS HIDING ANYTHING.
YOU JUST DIDN'T SAY IT BECAUSE YOU WERE NEVER ASKED?
RIGHT.
WAIT A MINUTE...ARE YOU SURE?
I THINK YOU JUST WANTED AN EXCUSE TO EXTEND THE DEADLINE FOR TELLING US EVERYTHING ABOUT YOURSELF.
IT SOUNDS COOL TO SAY, "WE ARE FINE, SINCE WE TRUST EACH OTHER."
BUT THE TRUTH IS IT'S A SCARY THOUGHT THAT YOU MIGHT BE HATED ONCE YOU REVEAL YOURSELF.
THAT'S ENOUGH!
?!
WHEN YOU GUYS ARE SO *SECRETIVE* ABOUT YOUR PASTS, I'VE GOT *NO* REASON TO OPEN UP TO *YOU*!
NONE!!
GOT IT?

I sound like I'm confessing my love for you.
I'M GOING TO REVEAL THINGS ABOUT MYSELF LITTLE BY LITTLE.
SO PLEASE FORGIVE ME THIS TIME.

...YOU MUST GIVE ME A KISS TO KEEP MY MOUTH SHUT TO ALZEID, OKAY?
YOU MEAN TO SILENCE YOU?

I'LL FORGIVE YOU FOR A MEAT BUN.
touch
GOOD! AND ALSO...

Silencing him.
RAHZEL?

ARE YOU GOING OUT?
YES. I NEED TO GO SHOP-PING.
IF YOU HAVE TIME, COULD YOU BE MY GUIDE?

SHE CAN GO EXPLORING **AFTER** I GIVE HER THIS MUFFLER I KNITTED OVERNIGHT.

PLEASE GIVE US A SECOND.

OVER-NIGHT?

HE KNIT-TED?

LISTEN! YOUR CURFEW IS FIVE P.M.! DINNER WILL BE FRIED SHRIMP!

I'LL MAKE IT **CRISPY** FOR YOU!

HE'S A GOOD FATHER.

I'M SO SORRY...

DON'T WORRY! YOU'RE NOT THE ONLY ONE WHO HAS A DOTING PARENT.
I'M SORRY.

LISTEN, LARAWELL...

THIS ISN'T HOMEWORK-- THIS IS AN ASSIGNMENT FROM NOW ON, OKAY?
TRY TO STOP SAYING SORRY TWO OUT OF EVERY THREE TIMES YOU OPEN YOUR MOUTH.
OKAY?

?!

AH HA HA! I DID IT!

I ATTACKED THE MONSTER!!

ARE YOU ALL RIGHT? LET ME SEE YOUR FOREHEAD.

WHAT WAS THAT?!

Oh no! You're bleeding!

IS THIS SOMETHING LIKE HOW WHEN A BOY'S AT A CERTAIN STAGE OF GROWTH, HE MAKES A GIRL CRY IF HE LIKES HER?

Eeek!

NO, THAT WAS GOING TOO FAR FOR THAT!

I'M GONNA CATCH HIM AND SHAVE HIS HEAD LIKE A REVERSE MOHAWK!

The reverse Mohawk.

IT'S OKAY! THIS HAPPENS TO ME ALL THE TIME!

Variations

ALL THE TIME?!

THAT'S EVEN *WORSE*!!

LET'S GO, WATSON!

WHO'S WATSON?! ME?!

OKAY, OKAY!

PLEASE WAIT...

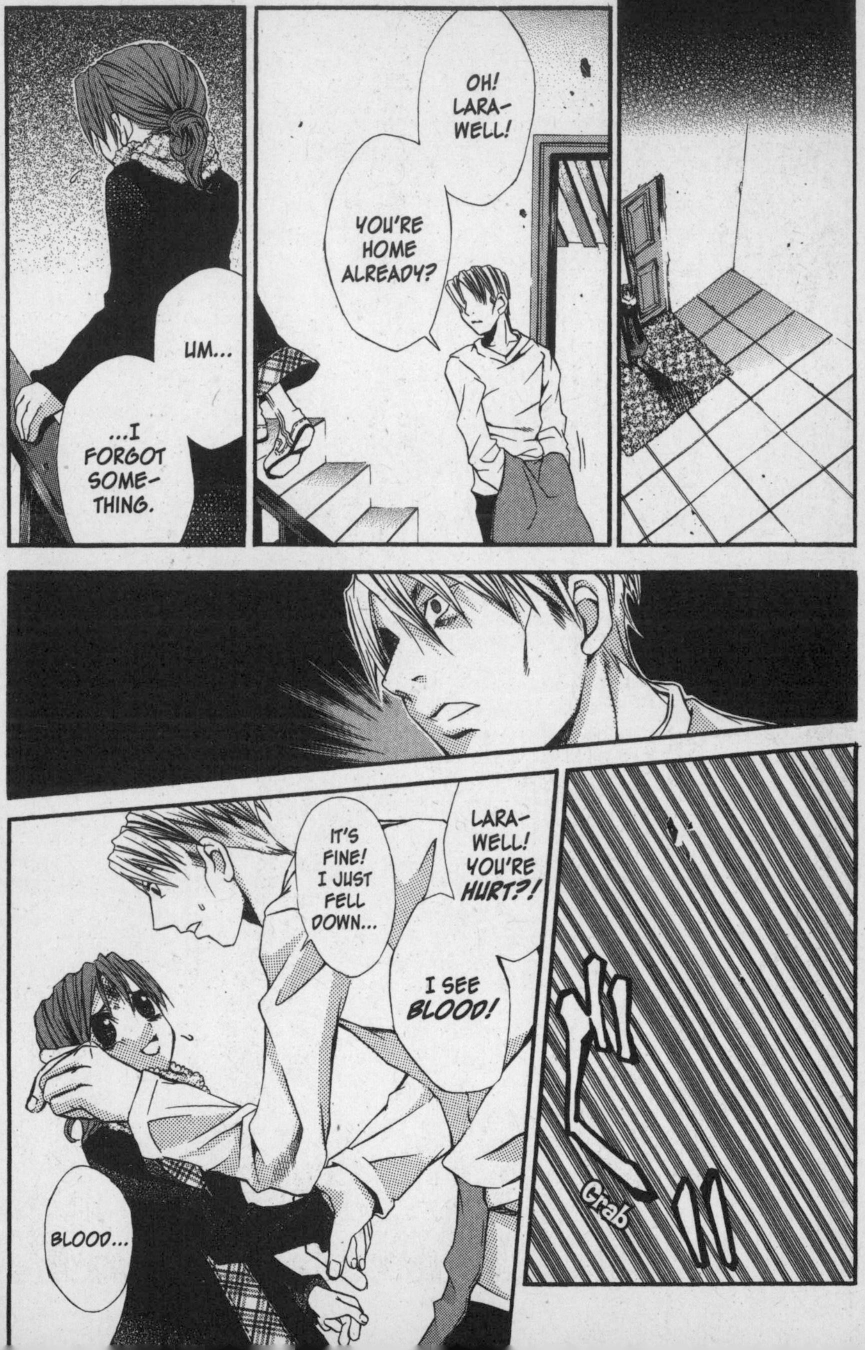

Grab

LARA-WELL! YOU'RE *HURT?!*

IT'S FINE! I JUST FELL DOWN...

I SEE *BLOOD!*

BLOOD...

BLOOD ...
BLOOD IS COMING DOWN...
IT'S RED...
BLOOOD!!
...RED...
IT'S FINE! PLEASE CALM DOWN, DADDY!

......
A bone?

IT'S SUCH BAD TASTE.

IT'S NOT THAT BAD.

IT LOOKS LIKE THE CRUCIFIXION OF CHRIST. I LIKE IT.
DON'T YOU THINK SO, ALZEID?
WHO THE HELL ARE YOU?
YES...
WHO INDEED?

I SAW SOME PEOPLE WITH HER TODAY...
...BUT I'M SURE THEY WON'T CHASE US FOR HER SAKE.
YAHOO! WE RULE!
DO YOU WANNA PLAY SOCCER WITH ME?

WHAT DID YOU SAY?!
ARE YOU STUPID?!
HEY... DON'T BE MEAN.
SOCCER IS FUN!
I'LL BE THE PLAYER...
...AND YOU GUYS ARE THE BALL!

THE BALL IS...
...MY FRIEND!!
Ugh!!

HAND!
WHAT?! DID I BREAK A RULE ALREADY?!
IT WAS GONNA BE MORE EXCITING THIS WAY!
Gwah!

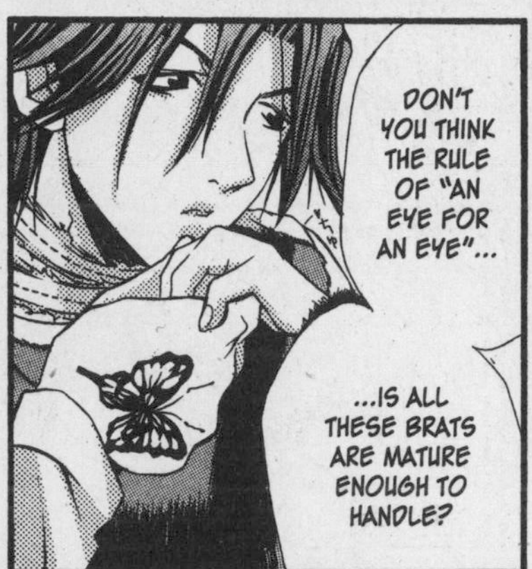
DON'T YOU THINK THE RULE OF "AN EYE FOR AN EYE"...
...IS ALL THESE BRATS ARE MATURE ENOUGH TO HANDLE?

THAT'S GOING TOO FAR.

I'M NOT SAYING YOU'RE WRONG.
BUT AN ADULT BEATING UP KIDS?
I DON'T WANT TO SEE THAT.

Noooo!!
YOU GOTTA TAKE OFF HIS PANTS WHEN YOU WANNA SMACK HIS BUTT!
You're too shy, Rahzel.
BUT I'M PRETTY GOOD AT PUNISHING KIDS.

HEY, DID YOU CHECK HOW LARAWELL WAS?

I HAVE NO IDEA.
YOU JUST LEFT HER OUT THERE?!
YOU'RE THE ONE WHO CALLED TO ME LIKE YOUR PET...
AND I RE-SPONDED, "WOOF WOOF!"

↑Baroqueheat was partially mind-controlled by Rahzel.

ANYWAY, I BETTER GO BACK TO HER!
CAN YOU COME WITH ME TO GO SHOPPING LATER?
OF COURSE.

LISTEN TO ME, KIDS!
YOU'D BETTER BE SWEET TO GIRLS FROM NOW ON, SO YOU CAN TASTE THEIR GOODNESS EARLIER! ♥
THAT GIRL IS DIFFER-ENT!

THAT GIRL IS A ***MONSTER***, SO WE CAN DO ANYTHING TO HER!

AND I'M GONNA FEED YOU TO THE BIRDS, TOO--JUST LIKE THE OTHER MONSTERS!

YOU SAY SHE'S A MONSTER...

CARE TO EXPLAIN WHY YOU CALL HER THAT?

IDIOT! I WON'T TELL YOU!

LISTEN...

I'M NOT GONNA GO EASY ON YOU JUST 'CAUSE YOU'RE KIDS.

ESPECIALLY NOT KIDS WHO ATTACK GIRLS.

THERE IS NO KIND WOMAN HERE TO STOP ME ANYMORE.

SO...WHAT SHOULD I DO WITH YOU NOW?

I'M HOME.

THOUGH, I GUESS IT'S NOT MY HOME.
But that's okay.
LARAWELL? ARE YOU HOME?

EIGHT YEARS AGO, HER MOTHER WAS PREGNANT AND GOT KILLED BY A ROBBER.

I HEARD SHE GOT STABBED A BUNCH OF TIMES WITH A KNIFE.

HER CORPSE WAS CRUCIFIED AND PUT IN THE SKY BURIAL.

IT WAS OBVIOUS THAT THE BABY WAS DEAD.

A FEW DAYS LATER, HER FATHER BROUGHT THIS NEWBORN BABY OUT OF NOWHERE.

ISN'T SHE CUTE? SHE'S MY BABY.
AND PEOPLE WHO STAYED AT HIS HOTEL HAVE BEEN FOUND DEAD EVER SINCE THEN.
THAT MAN SOLD HIS SOUL TO THE DEVIL.
ADULTS WERE SAYING IT WAS BLACK MAGIC.
THEY SAID ALL THE DEAD PEOPLE WERE SACRIFICED BY HIM.
THAT'S STRANGE.
NOBODY'S HERE?
Step

HE SOLD HIS SOUL TO THE DEVIL, AND...
WHAT'S GOING ON HERE?
IS ANYBODY HOME?

Chapter 15:
The Sun in the Palm--Part 4: A Break in the Clouds

WELCOME HOME.

ALZEID!

WE'RE LEAVING THIS TOWN RIGHT AWAY.
WHAT? RIGHT THIS SECOND? WHY?!

I DON'T KNOW.
I HAVE NO CLUE WHAT RUNS THROUGH THAT HEAD OF YOURS!
I DON'T EVEN KNOW WHAT YOU EAT AND HOW IT'S DIGESTED AND HOW IT WORKS FOR YOUR PHYSIOLOGY!

WE HAVEN'T PAID THE HOTEL BILL YET, AND BAROQUEHEAT IS STILL IN TOWN!

I LEFT SOME MONEY IN THE ROOM, SINCE I COULDN'T FIND THE HOTEL OWNER.

AND I CAN EDUCATE YOU BETTER WITHOUT BAROQUEHEAT AROUND.

BUT WHY ARE WE LEAVING RIGHT NOW?
BECAUSE I SAY SO.

YOU'D BETTER THREATEN OR BEG ME IF YOU EXPECT ME TO DO WHAT YOU WANT!
WHERE ARE YOU GOING?!

?!
IDIOT!

I HAVEN'T FINISHED SHOPPING YET!
DIDN'T YOU ORDER ME TO DO IT?! STUPID!
Tsk
DO YOU KNOW ABOUT THE CRIMINAL GENE THEORY?

IT SAYS THERE'S CRIMINAL BEHAVIOR PRO-GRAMMED INTO A CRIMINAL'S BODY FROM THE VERY BEGIN-NING.
ISN'T THAT FASCINAT-ING?

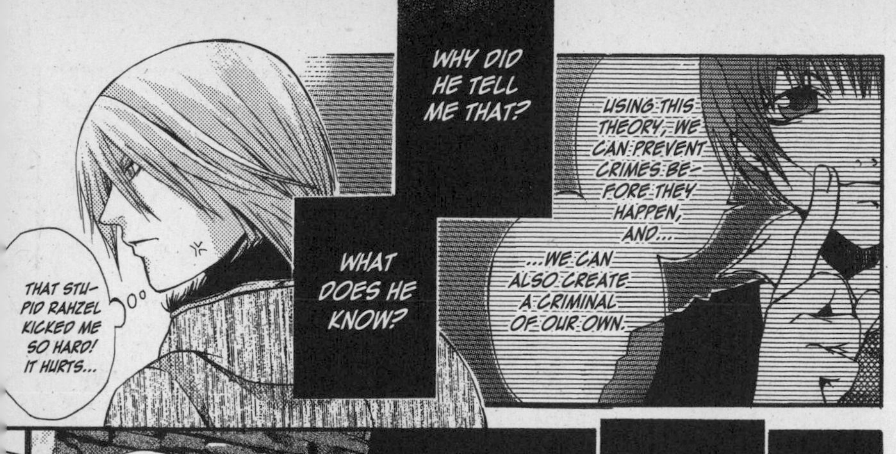

USING THIS THEORY, WE CAN PREVENT CRIMES BEFORE THEY HAPPEN, AND...
...WE CAN ALSO CREATE A CRIMINAL OF OUR OWN.
WHY DID HE TELL ME THAT?
WHAT DOES HE KNOW?
THAT STUPID RAHZEL KICKED ME SO HARD! IT HURTS...

ANYWAY, I DON'T LIKE WHAT'S GOING ON RIGHT NOW!
Restaurant
RAHZEL, ARE YOU IN A BAD MOOD?

NOT REALLY.

I'M IN A TOTALLY GREAT MOOD.

うぐうぐ

DOES THAT TASTE GOOD?

IT'S DELICIOUS. ♡

BY THE WAY, I FOUND OUT ABOUT LARAWELL'S MOTHER.

That's good, then.

SHE WAS STABBED TO DEATH BY A ROBBER.

SHE WAS STABBED SO BADLY THAT LARAWELL, WHO SHE WAS STILL PREGNANT WITH, WAS PRESUMED DEAD.
?
BUT SHE'S ALIVE, ISN'T SHE?

SHE WAS BROUGHT BACK TO LIFE.
HUH?
WHAT I HEARD WAS...

BLACK MAGIC?!

WHY WOULD SHE SUDDENLY BE REBORN WITH BLACK MAGIC?
I DON'T KNOW.

I GUESS SOME DEAD BODIES WERE DISCOVERED, AND THEY DIDN'T LOOK NORMAL.
SO THE TOWNSPEOPLE ARE TRYING TO RELATE IT TO LARAWELL OR SOMETHING.

HOW WEREN'T THEY NORMAL?!
WELL, THE BODIES WERE CUT INTO PIECES, AND SOMEONE DREW SOMETHING ON THEM WITH BLOOD.
WHOA! I JUST TOTALLY LOST MY APPETITE!
BY THE WAY, CAN I GET SOME MORE PASTA?

IT SOUNDS STUPID.
WOULDN'T IT MAKE MORE SENSE TO BRING HER MOM BACK TO LIFE FIRST?
IT MIGHT HAVE BEEN MORE CONVENIENT TO LEAVE HER DEAD.
WHAT DO YOU MEAN...?
I'M JUST BOUNCING IDEAS OFF YOU.
ANYWAY, IT'S IMPOSSIBLE FOR A DEAD PERSON TO COME BACK TO LIFE.
SHE PROBABLY GAVE BIRTH RIGHT BEFORE HER DEATH.
GYAAAHH!!
WHAT'S WITH THE RUCKUS?! YOU'RE DISTURBING THE CUSTOMERS!
L-L-L-
LOOK AT THAT!

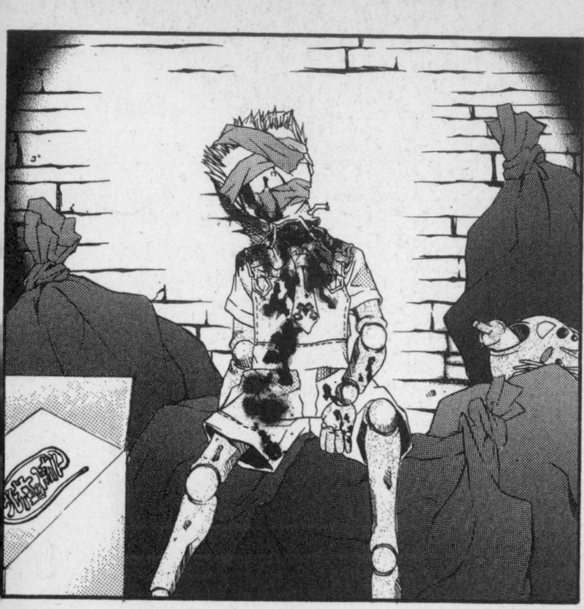

WELCOME BACK!
?

WHAT'S WRONG? YOU LOOK UNSETTLED.
......
THIS AFTER-NOON...

WHERE...
WHERE WERE YOU THIS AFTER-NOON?

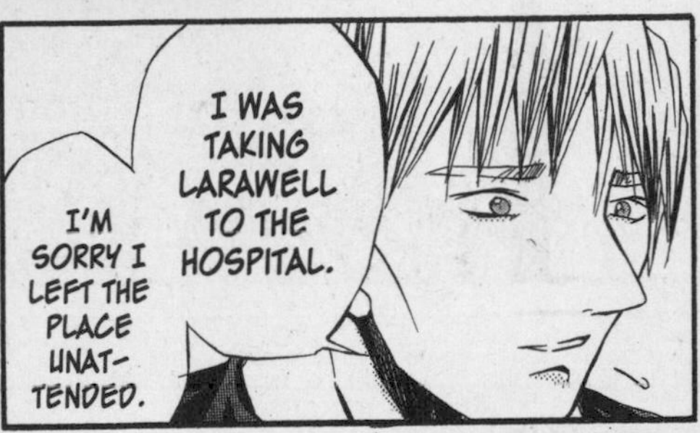
I WAS TAKING LARAWELL TO THE HOSPITAL.
I'M SORRY I LEFT THE PLACE UNAT-TENDED.

THAT'S OKAY.
I WAS JUST WORRIED.
JENFOUPE!!

YOU FINALLY KILLED SOME-ONE IN OUR TOWN!

WHAT ARE YOU TALKING ABOUT?
What's going on?
QUIT ACTING!
SOMEONE SAW YOU WANDERING AROUND THE TOWN TODAY!

AS LONG AS IT WAS JUST YOUR HOTEL GUESTS YOU WERE KILLING, WE TURNED A BLIND EYE. BUT NOW YOU'VE KILLED ONE OF OUR TOWNS-PEOPLE!

PLEASE STOP! THERE MUST BE A MISTAKE!

OUT OF MY WAY!

IF YOU TRY TO PROTECT HIM, YOU'LL BE CHARGED AS AN ACCOMPLICE!

OH YEAH, YOU!

YOU SHARE THE BLOOD OF A KILLER!

OOPS!

I SLIPPED!

ARE YOU GOING TO INTERRUPT US NOW, OUTSIDER?!

THAT'S RIGHT! VIOLENCE DOESN'T SOLVE ANYTHING!

THAT WASN'T JUST INTERRUPTING! THAT WAS KICKING!!

YOU'RE WEARING PLATFORMS ALREADY, AREN'T YOU?

IGNORING

DO ME A FAVOR AND CUT OFF YOUR HEIGHT FOR ME.

It's only fair.

MAYBE CUT OFF YOUR HEAD.

I CAN'T CUT OFF MY HEAD!

LARAWELL ISN'T REALLY MY CHILD.

I FOUND HER AS AN ABANDONED BABY AT THE GRAVE WHERE MY WIFE WAS CRUCIFIED.

YOU CAN IMAGINE WHAT HAPPENED AFTER THAT.

WELL... I DO HAVE ONE MORE THING TO CONFESS.

EIGHT YEARS AGO, I WAS THE ONE WHO KILLED MY WIFE, TOO.

JENFOUPE, I WANT A DIVORCE.

I AM SO SORRY, LARA-WELL...
I CAN'T THINK OF ANYTHING THAT I CAN DO FOR YOU ANYMORE.
EEEEEEK!!
WAAAH!!!
Clomp
RAHZEL?
ARE YOU THINKING ABOUT LARAWELL?
......
YEAH...
I WONDER IF I SHOULD HAVE STAYED ONE MORE DAY FOR HER.

AND THE DAY AFTER THAT, YOU'D WANT TO STAY YET ANOTHER DAY?
WHEN YOU KNOW YOU CAN'T BE WITH HER FOR-EVER, IT DOESN'T MATTER WHETHER IT'S TODAY OR TOMORROW THAT YOU LEAVE.
I STILL CAN'T BE-LIEVE HER FATHER WAS THE KILLER.

......

RAHZEL?
THINK ABOUT IT! HE JUST HAD TO KILL THE PEOPLE WHO HARMED LARAWELL!
WHY DID HE HAVE TO PIECE THAT CORPSE BACK TOGETHER AND SHOW IT OFF ON PURPOSE?

BASICALLY, YOU'RE SAYING THAT...
...HE DEFLECTED ATTENTION FROM THE TRUE KILLER BY CREATING DIS-TURBING ARTWORK OUT OF CORPSES, SPOTLIGHTING HIMSELF.
HE FINALLY KILLED HIM-SELF, STILL LIVING THE LIE EVEN AT THE END.
AS AWKWARD AS IT MAY BE, I'M SURE ALL THE TOWNSPEOPLE ARE JUST RELIEVED THAT HE'S DEAD.

DON'T YOU UNDER-STAND?
THERE'S ONLY ONE PERSON HE WOULD PROTECT BY PLAYING SUCH A ROLE.
I KNOW THAT!!

YOU WERE SAYING SOMETHING INTERESTING EARLIER.
IF I EXPECT YOU TO DO WHAT I WANT...HOW DID THAT GO AGAIN?

IF YOU REFUSE ME THIS, I'LL MAKE ONLY CARROTS AND GREEN PEPPERS FOR YOUR MEALS FROM NOW ON.
YOU ARE TRULY EVIL.

THAT'S WHY I WANT TO CHECK ONE MORE TIME.
I WANT TO MAKE SURE I'M JUST IMAGINING THINGS.
CAN'T I GO BACK...?

CLOSED

LARA-WELL?
ARE YOU HOME?

THERE'S NO ANSWER.

SHE MIGHT BE SLEEPING BY NOW.

OPTION ONE--BREAK THROUGH THE WINDOWS. OPTION TWO--BREAK DOWN THE DOOR. OPTION THREE--BREAK EVERYTHING.

PICK ONE!

slip

WHY ARE THOSE THE ONLY OPTIONS?!

YOU'RE A BORN CRIMINAL.

RAHZEL...

THIS MAN TRIED TO KILL ME...
HE SAID IT WAS REVENGE FOR HIS DEAD SON.

DO YOU THINK IT WILL BE CONSIDERED SELF-DE-FENSE?
AH HA HA...

MAY I ASK YOU A QUESTION?
I AM A MURDERER. DOES THAT MAKE YOU FEEL DISGUSTED?

I WAS ONLY FOUR THE FIRST TIME I KILLED SOMEONE.

HE WAS ONE OF THE GUESTS AT OUR HOTEL.
ASHES FROM HIS CIGARETTE FELL ON ME WHEN HE WAS PASSING BY.
IT WAS PAINFUL.

I'M NOT DISGUSTED...
...BUT I DON'T UNDER-STAND IT.

AND THAT WAS IT. THAT WAS THE ONLY REASON...
DOESN'T IT SOUND INSANE? I'VE ALREADY KILLED SEVEN PEOPLE FOR SUCH STUPID REASONS.

I DON'T KNOW WHY I DO THINGS LIKE THAT.
I DON'T *WANT* TO KILL ANYONE.
I'VE NEVER HATED ANYONE IN MY LIFE, EITHER.

LARA-WELL...
Bang!
PLEASE DON'T COME NEAR ME!!
Sshk!
DO YOU REMEMBER...
...THE HOMEWORK?
HOMEWORK...
!!
ARE YOU SCARED OF ME? ARE YOU DISGUSTED BY ME?
NO...
WHY?
THAT IS... I MEAN...
I'LL TELL YOU THE ANSWER NOW.

IT'S BECAUSE YOUR HAND ON MY FACE WAS SO WARM...
IT WAS WARM LIKE SUN-SHINE...
NOOOOOO!!
Splat!

LARA-WELL!!
HOLD STILL, IDIOT!!
NO!
NOOOOO! LET GO OF ME!!
CALM DOWN. THERE'S NOTHING YOU CAN DO FOR HER.
THINK OF YOUR-SELF.
THIS WOUND ISN'T HURTING OR BUGGING ME AT ALL!
I HAVE TO HURRY AND HELP LARAWELL BEFORE--
SHUT UP!!

I couldn't reach her...
W-WHY...?!

WHY CAN'T MY HAND HOLD ON TO ANYTHING...

...WHEN IT MOST NEEDS TO...?

I couldn't read...

...the eyes and hands that seek help...

IT HURTS!

IT HURTS SO MUCH!!

PLEASE HELP HER...!!

PLEASE HELP HER, ALZEID!!

WHAT'S THAT?
IT'S A BAL-LOON.
I CAN SEE IT'S A BALLOON!

AND EVENTUALLY, THE REAL BIRD WILL POKE THE BALLOON, AND IT'LL CRASH.
Its life will be short.
DON'T YOU EVER SAY THAT AGAIN!!

LARAWELL ONCE TOLD ME THAT SHE WANTED TO FLY LIKE A BIRD...
I JUST WANTED TO SEND MY WISH UP FOR HER.

WHY ARE YOU JUST STANDING THERE, STUPID CHICK?
LET'S GO!
ALL RIGHT, ALL RIGHT...

C'MON.

THE WEATHER'S SO NICE!
IT'S SUCH A GREAT SUNNY AUTUMN DAY!
IT'S WINTER. FACE REALITY.
THEN, IT'S A SUNNY WINTER AUTUMN DAY!
YOU GUYS NEED TO GO BACK TO ELEMENTARY SCHOOL!
Dazzle Volume 2 END

Dazzle Q&A

We'll be waiting for your questions...

Chapter 8: Nowhere to Go–Part 3: Like Praying

Baroqueheat is so young here! He's even childlike! I must admit to myself again that I can't draw men well. Should I just change all the male characters to transsexuals and make it a yuri manga?! I can make it the love comedy of girly Alzeid-chan and Baroqueheat-chan battling over Rahzel. They fight against the evil school organization! (I'm losing myself here.) But they have thick bone structures, so they can't be girls, so I fear I must reject this idea.

Chapter 9: Nowhere to Go–Part 4: Broken Wings

In the postscript to Volume 1, I explained my horror experience of hearing noises from the stereo without it being plugged in. After that I got a bunch of letters from the readers, and they gave me some good advice...but I had to admit something was in my house when I saw a white hand coming out of my pillow!! (Crying.) Nothing bad happened to me or anything (the hand was just waving), but I was so petrified with horror I couldn't move! So I decided to watch whatever was on TV, but they were just showing some boring golf tournament!! That really, really pissed me off for the rest of the day! It was my fault that I was sleeping on a Saturday afternoon, but I would feel better if the ghosts would only come out at night...

Chapter 10: Nowhere to Go–Part 5: Quiet Rain

And now for something completely different--I think it's too difficult to wear a long skirt in the rain. Leather shoes get destroyed in the rain, too. One must wear a raincoat and rain boots in wet weather!

Intermission: Morning Scenery

When this story was published in the magazine, it was between Chapter 8 and Chapter 9. Come to think of it, Alzeid didn't appear much within those two months! Keep working hard, Alzeid!! (For what?)

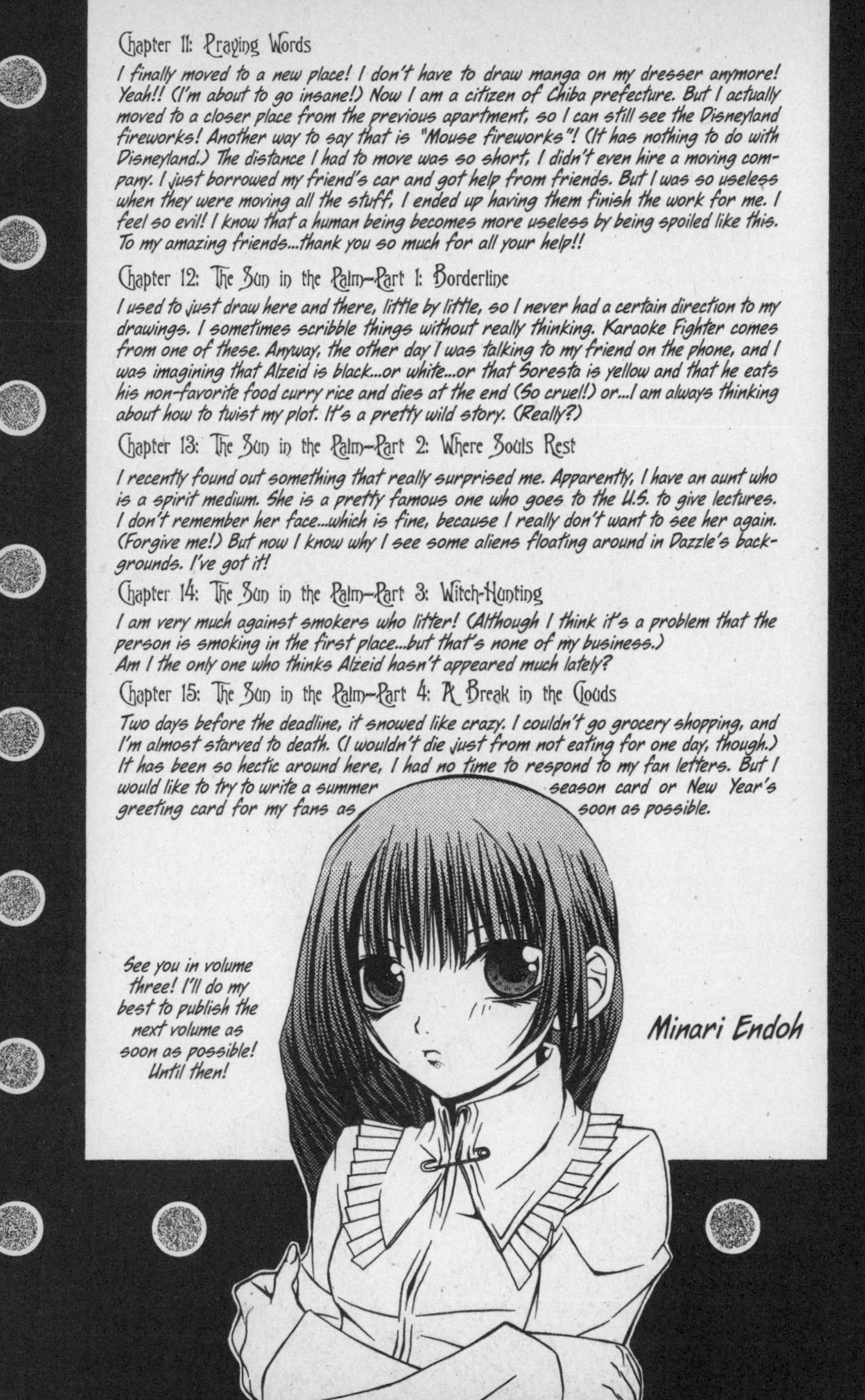

Chapter 11: Praying Words

I finally moved to a new place! I don't have to draw manga on my dresser anymore! Yeah!! (I'm about to go insane!) Now I am a citizen of Chiba prefecture. But I actually moved to a closer place from the previous apartment, so I can still see the Disneyland fireworks! Another way to say that is "Mouse fireworks"! (It has nothing to do with Disneyland.) The distance I had to move was so short, I didn't even hire a moving company. I just borrowed my friend's car and got help from friends. But I was so useless when they were moving all the stuff, I ended up having them finish the work for me. I feel so evil! I know that a human being becomes more useless by being spoiled like this. To my amazing friends...thank you so much for all your help!!

Chapter 12: The Sun in the Palm—Part 1: Borderline

I used to just draw here and there, little by little, so I never had a certain direction to my drawings. I sometimes scribble things without really thinking. Karaoke Fighter comes from one of these. Anyway, the other day I was talking to my friend on the phone, and I was imagining that Alzeid is black...or white...or that Soresta is yellow and that he eats his non-favorite food curry rice and dies at the end (So cruel!) or...I am always thinking about how to twist my plot. It's a pretty wild story. (Really?)

Chapter 13: The Sun in the Palm—Part 2: Where Souls Rest

I recently found out something that really surprised me. Apparently, I have an aunt who is a spirit medium. She is a pretty famous one who goes to the U.S. to give lectures. I don't remember her face...which is fine, because I really don't want to see her again. (Forgive me!) But now I know why I see some aliens floating around in Dazzle's backgrounds. I've got it!

Chapter 14: The Sun in the Palm—Part 3: Witch-Hunting

I am very much against smokers who litter! (Although I think it's a problem that the person is smoking in the first place...but that's none of my business.)
Am I the only one who thinks Alzeid hasn't appeared much lately?

Chapter 15: The Sun in the Palm—Part 4: A Break in the Clouds

Two days before the deadline, it snowed like crazy. I couldn't go grocery shopping, and I'm almost starved to death. (I wouldn't die just from not eating for one day, though.) It has been so hectic around here, I had no time to respond to my fan letters. But I would like to try to write a summer season card or New Year's greeting card for my fans as soon as possible.

See you in volume three! I'll do my best to publish the next volume as soon as possible! Until then!

Minari Endoh

height 182cm
weight 63kg
eyecolor scarlet
haircolor white
likes
cocoa
peach
sweets
sleep
dislikes
morning
bath
alarm
carrot
greenpepper

When Rahzel, Alzeid and Baroqueheat arrive in a new town, they run into an old acquaintance of Rahzel's named Jelice... who gives the boys some interesting insight into Rahzel's past. Meanwhile, the town's local religious leader becomes obsessed with Rahzel...to the point of actually kidnapping her! Just what nefarious plans does he have in store for our sojourning sorceress?
Find out in Volume 3 of Dazzle!

SHRINE OF THE MORNING MIST

BY HIROKI UGAWA

When the spirit world suddenly shifts out of balance, it's up to sisters Kurako, Yuzu and Tama to save us—but first they must get through their family drama.

CONFIDENTIAL CONFESSIONS -DEAI-

BY REIKO MOMOCHI

In this unflinching portrayal of teens in crisis, silence isn't always golden…

DEATH JAM

BY JEON SANG YOUNG

Muchaca Smooth is an assassin with just one shot to make it big!

ROZEN MAIDEN

BY PEACH-PIT

Welcome to the world of *Rozen Maiden* where a boy must enter an all-new reality to protect and serve a living doll!

From the creators of *DearS*!

BOYS OF SUMMER

BY CHUCK AUSTEN AND HIROKI OTSUKA

Just because you strike out on your first attempt at scoring with a girl doesn't mean you won't end up hitting a home run!

KAT & MOUSE

BY ALEX DE CAMPI AND FEDERICA MANFREDI

When science whiz Kat teams up with computer nerd Mouse, bullies and blackmailers don't stand a chance!

TOKYOPOP PRESENTS

For Believers...

Scrapped Princess: A Tale of Destiny

By Ichiro Sakaki

A dark prophecy reveals that the queen will give birth to a daughter who will usher in the Apocalypse. But despite all attempts to destroy the baby, the myth of the "Scrapped Princess" lingers on...

THE INSPIRATION FOR THE HIT ANIME AND MANGA SERIES!

For Thinkers...

Kino no Tabi: Book One of The Beautiful World

By Keiichi Sigsawa

Kino roams the world on the back of Hermes, her unusual motorcycle, in a journey filled with happiness and pain, decadence and violence, and magic and loss.

THE SENSATIONAL BESTSELLER IN JAPAN HAS FINALLY ARRIVED!

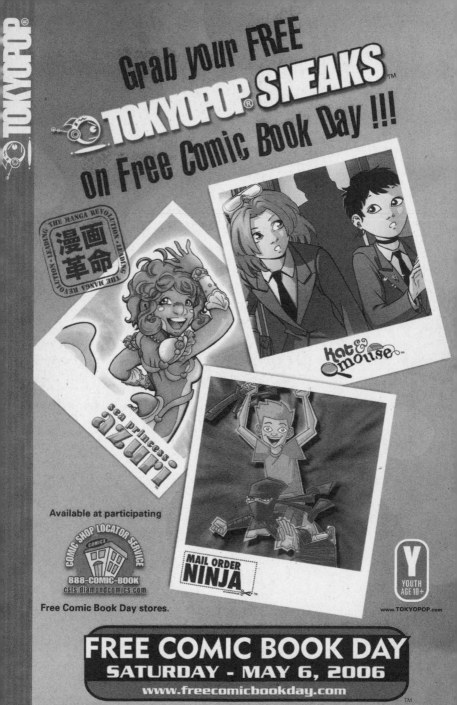

that I'm not like other people...

STOP!

This is the back of the book.
You wouldn't want to spoil a great ending!

This book is printed "manga-style," in the authentic Japanese right-to-left format. Since none of the artwork has been flipped or altered, readers get to experience the story just as the creator intended. You've been asking for it, so TOKYOPOP® delivered: authentic, hot-off-the-press, and far more fun!

DIRECTIONS

If this is your first time reading manga-style, here's a quick guide to help you understand how it works.

It's easy... just start in the top right panel and follow the numbers. Have fun, and look for more 100% authentic manga from TOKYOPOP®!